New shopping in historic towns:
the Chesterfield story

English ⌗ Heritage

New shopping in historic towns: the Chesterfield story

Tony Aldous

report commissioned by English Heritage

1990

Copyright © 1990 English Heritage

Published 1990 by English Heritage
Fortress House, 23 Savile Row,
London W1X 1AB

ISBN 1 85074 298 7

British Library Cataloguing in Publication Data
Aldous, Tony
   New shopping in historic towns : the Chesterfield story.
   1. Derbyshire. Chesterfield. Shopping facilities. Planning
   I. Title   II. English Heritage *Historic Areas Division*
   711.55220942512

   ISBN 1–85074–298–7

Printed in the United Kingdom by
Hobbs the Printers of Southampton SO9 2UZ

Contents

Frontispiece: Market Place on market day

Introduction

A previous volume under the title *Conservation in Action – Chester's Bridgegate* was published by Her Majesty's Stationery Office in 1982. Prepared by Donald W Insall & Associates and the Department of the Environment's Directorate of Ancient Monuments and Historic Buildings, it described the coordinated programme to conserve and revitalise the Bridgegate area of Chester.

Chesterfield is very different from Chester. It has fewer historic buildings, has not traditionally been regarded as a prime tourist destination, is a much more workaday industrial town, and by the mid 1970s had suffered almost two decades of economic decline which, as some saw it, threatened to become irreversible.

But in view of what subsequently happened, Chesterfield is a most appropriate subject for a successor to the *Chester* volume. For having tried unsuccessfully to use comprehensive redevelopment as a means to revitalise the town centre, the Borough Council was – in the nick of time – persuaded to try instead what we may call 'coordinated conservation'.

It worked. Chesterfield as a shopping centre is today thriving, and it is, to the wonder of many of its inhabitants, well on the way to becoming a popular tourist destination. Its people feel a new pride of place and share the enthusiasm of outsiders for what has been achieved.

As at Chester, one major reason for success was the appointment of conservation consultants, at the urging of the Historic Buildings Council and 50% paid for by the Department of the Environment. As at Chester, the role of those consultants, architect-planners, Feilden & Mawson, is a continuing and vital one, bringing a fresh but experienced eye to what had become 'ingrowing' problems.

English Heritage, having assumed the mantle of the HBC and the Directorate in relation to Chesterfield, believed that the experience of 'conservation in action' in this more workaday setting was worth describing and worth trying to draw lessons from.

As work on this volume has progressed, the boom in retail development has reached unprecedented heights. Its dangers have led English Heritage to produce a set of guidelines for shopping development in historic towns. Chesterfield's experience in integrating shopping with conservation is now visible for all to see; like the guidelines it provides useful lessons for those with the wit to learn from them. A summary of the more important lessons appears in chapter 8.

Perhaps the central lesson to be stressed is this. Both shopkeeping and shopping development are today more competitive than they have ever been. That competition is not simply in goods, but in attractive shopping environments. Today's shoppers are very choosy about this: bland, climate-controlled malls tend to 'turn them off'. They want convenient, pleasant places but also places with distinctive, authentic character.

To command and retain shopper loyalty, therefore, a successful shopping centre needs to build on the kind of characteristics that have made Chesterfield a commercial and popular success. The conservation-oriented upgrading of existing town centres is a sound long-term investment, not only for councils and communities but increasingly for developers.

1 A town in need of new life

What kind of town?

Chesterfield is not a York, a Bath, or even a Chester. It has few outstanding buildings and, until the mid 1970s, that meant few listed buildings. Two features, however, have always struck visitors as memorable: the Crooked Spire of St Mary and All Saints Church, and the market square with its thrice weekly open market (Fig 1).

The crooked spire of St Mary's is one of Derbyshire's best-known landmarks. There has been a church on the site at least since the time of Edward the Confessor (1042–66). The oldest part of the present building dates from the thirteenth century; the tower and the south transept were added in the fourteenth (Fig 2).

In that century also the 70m (228ft) octagonal spire was added. Given the materials available, it was a daring piece of construction. The twist seems to have been the result of the heat of the sun on green timber which split. But despite its 2.6m (8ft 7in) lean, which makes it look as if it is always about to fall, the Crooked Spire is quite stable.

Chesterfield has had a market to certain knowledge almost as long as it has had a church. King John granted a right of market in 1204 to the then lord of the manor, one William Brewer. That seems to have been nearer the church, but it later moved to open ground to the west where

Fig 1 High Street looking towards the parish church of St Mary and All Saints

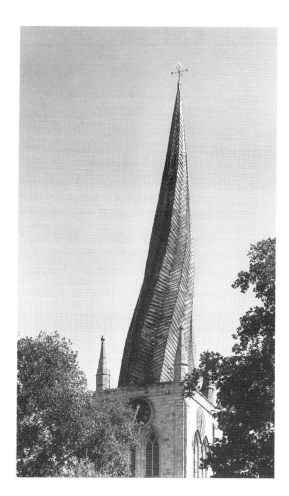

Fig 2   The famous twisted spire, St Mary and All Saints

the present market is – probably to give more room as trade increased.

That most famous of seventeenth-century tourists, Celia Fiennes, wrote:

> Chesterfield looks low when you approach it from the adjacent hill which you descend but then you ascend another to it; the Coal pits and quarries of stone are all about even just at the town end, and in the town its all built of stone; the church stands in a place of eminency, the town looks well, the Streets good the Market very large; it was Saturday which is their market day and there was a great Market like some little faire. In this town is the best ale in the kingdom generally esteem'd.

Daniel Defoe, in the early eighteenth century, also visited Chesterfield. He found it 'a handsome populous town, well built and well inhabited' but added, 'Here, however, is nothing remarkable in this town, but a free school and a very good market, well stored with provisions.'

Though customs and commodities change, Chesterfield's open market remained its social and commercial focus – a lively, colourful hubbub of stalls, shoppers, and traders. It was – and still is – probably the largest open market in the north of England (Figs 3–8).

Yet for more than a decade in the 1960s and early 1970s Chesterfield Borough Council, supported by Derbyshire County Council, seemed intent on destroying this open market place by covering it with an enclosed shopping centre. Successive council-backed schemes proposed to tidy the market traders away into a remote and antiseptic new market hall, leaving only a minority of stallholders operating in the open, in a small, draughty, and largely sunless square at the western end of the development.

The council's clear and uncompromising determination that this should come to pass unleashed the biggest controversy in Chesterfield's recent history. How was it that the councillors judged this drastic course to be in the town's and the citizens' best interest? And how did they – happily – come to change their minds?

Fig 3   Ordnance Survey Plan of the town centre in 1898

Fig 4   Market Place *c* 1890 looking north

Fig 5   Market Place. September Fair, 1882

Fig 6   Low Pavement. Demonstration, *c* 1890

Fig 7   Market Place. East frontage, *c* 1910

Fig 8   Central Pavement looking east towards Packers Row, *c* 1900

Clear-and-rebuild

During the 1960s many towns, large and small, concluded that their shopping centres were out-of-date and not performing well. Their classic dilemma was that the dual town centre functions of market place and traffic crossroads were no longer compatible. Increasing motor traffic and the narrow pavements of traditional high streets now provided shopping conditions that were neither agreeable nor efficient.

So, armed with new planning powers which allowed them to assemble sites for redevelopment, an increasing number of local authorities sought to create new, traffic-free, covered, and often air-conditioned shopping centres. They generally did so in partnership with a property developer and/or a financial institution, such as a pension fund or insurance company with funds to invest.

Chesterfield Town Map

In Chesterfield the story starts with the preparation of the Derbyshire County Development Plan in 1952, and its Chesterfield Town Map, circulated in draft in 1955 and submitted for ministerial approval in 1960.

Surveys made for the Town Map indicated a need to redevelop and revitalise the centre of Chesterfield. Little had changed since the creation in 1923 of Knifesmithgate and its tall mock-Tudor shop buildings on an east–west alignment north of the Market Place and High Street. Vehicle congestion was increasing; many buildings were obsolete and inefficient (Fig 9).

The Town Map proposed comprehensive redevelopment of the town centre: new roads, car parks, bus station, and a rebuilt Market Hall. It did not say in detail how this was to be achieved; that was to come later through the medium of amendments to the Town Map.

The plan takes shape

In 1956 Chesterfield Borough Council, like many other local authorities, began to think in terms of investment by a development company as its best means of achieving redevelopment. The council asked shopping consultants Goddard & Smith to advise on the state of shopping in their town and where new shops should be established.

Shopping had tended in recent years to move away from the Market Square eastwards along the High Street. Goddard & Smith's advice was that any new shops should be on the market place extending the High Street's southern frontage.

The acceptance of that advice by both borough and county councils was the main reason for the protracted and often bitter battle which followed.

The Allen plan

The borough council appointed a professor of architecture, J S Allen of Newcastle-upon-Tyne, to prepare a scheme along these lines. His proposals, published in 1962, were ambitious and wide-ranging (Figs 10, 11). They took in not only the Market Place, Market Hall, and New Square beyond it, but The Shambles – an area of narrow lanes and alleys – to the east and Low and Central Pavements to the south.

On this 2 hectare (5 acre) site Professor Allen envisaged 80 shops with a gross floor area of some 21,650 sq m (233,000 sq ft), 6200 sq m (66,680 sq ft) of market space, 2630 sq m (28,300 sq ft) of other commercial accommodation, and 2450 sq m (26,400 sq ft) of offices in a five-storey block intended for government departments, extendable to eleven storeys if needed. He proposed a multi-storey car park between New Beetwell Street and Markham Road (to the south of Low Pavement), with a new bus station alongside.

The plan followed the strategy suggested by the shopping consultants. It proposed, by building over the Market Place, to create

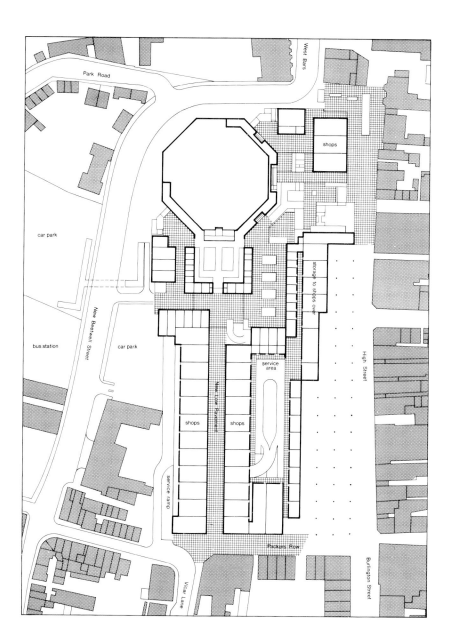
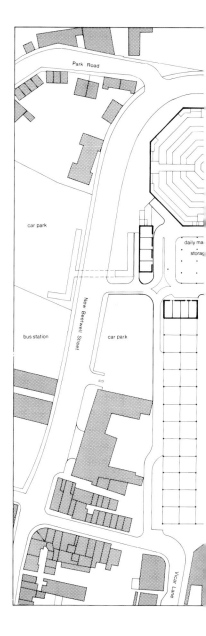

Fig 10 Scheme for a major shopping and office development covering Market Place, Low Pavement, Central Pavement, and The Shambles: prepared in 1962 by Professor J S Allen for Chesterfield Borough Council. Market Hall level, Mall level, and High Street level

CHESTERFIELD

town centre

0   100   200m

Fig 9   The town centre prior to major redevelopment

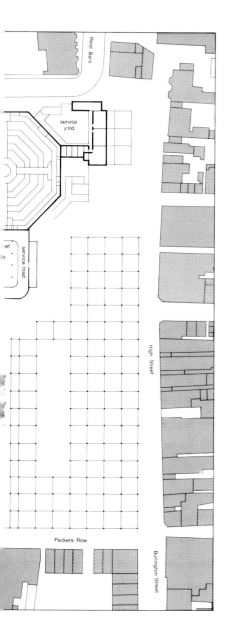

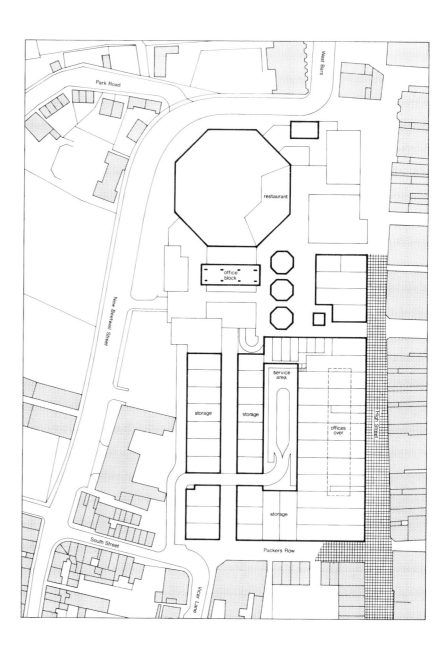

Fig 11   Sketch of Professor Allen's scheme

new shopping frontages in both High Street and Low Pavement. The majority of market traders were to move to a new, two-storey, octagonal building at the south-western corner of the site, with a small open market between it and the new shops.

In Chesterfield, as elsewhere at that time, public reaction was not over-critical. People were for the most part bemused rather than enthused. The man and woman in the street had not yet learned to be sceptical about cleansweep blueprints for New Jerusalems, nor had they yet experienced the disruptive and disorienting effect of large-scale demolition followed (by no means always immediately) by the 'Anywhere' 1960s style of redevelopment.

Choosing a partner

Partnership agreements with developers were at that time a method of achieving redevelopment recommended by the Ministry of Housing and Local Government. The MHLG's advocacy of this approach was spelled out in its 1962 Planning Bulletin, *Town centres: an approach to renewal*.

The borough council therefore sought a developer to join in the shopping and offices elements of the scheme. It received offers from ten companies, interviewed three of them, and in April 1965 chose the Hammerson Group, who were already involved in shopping developments in a number of towns. By December 1967 the council and the company had signed an agreement to build the Allen scheme, subject to planning permission being obtained.

From the early 1960s onwards work had also been proceeding on plans for the wider restructuring of the town centre, including redevelopment of obsolescent buildings as well as new roads and car parks. To achieve redevelopment, the council proposed three comprehensive development areas (CDAs): the Market Place with some adjoining properties, the Holywell Street/Saltergate area, and the Beetwell Street area. A non-statutory Town Centre Map spelled out how the local authority proposed to reorganise traffic, car parking, and

13

pedestrian circulation and also provided the context for the more detailed CDA proposals (Fig 12).

In 1967 Derbyshire County Council on the Borough Council's behalf submitted amendments to the (statutory) Chesterfield Town Map to the Minister along with the three CDAs and associated compulsory purchase orders. The Minister then predictably appointed an inspector to hold a public inquiry.

Opposition builds up

It was then that the – quite unpredicted – scale and breadth of developing opposition became apparent. The inquiry, which began in December 1967, had before it 204 objections and lasted 32 working days. Since what was at issue was a wholesale reshaping of the town centre, that was hardly surprising. The proposals would involve a huge investment and, people were increasingly coming to realise, enormous upheaval.

They were also becoming aware of what had happened in the redeveloped centres of other towns. As Chesterfield Civic Society's vice-chairman, Archdeacon T W Ingram Cleasy, put it in his evidence to the inquiry, 'We have no wish to see the ancient borough of Chesterfield reduced to the status of urban nonentity – no matter how modern.'

Fig 12 Plan prepared *c* 1965 by Derbyshire County Council in consultation with Chesterfield Borough Council showing areas proposed for comprehensive redevelopment and new and widened road proposals

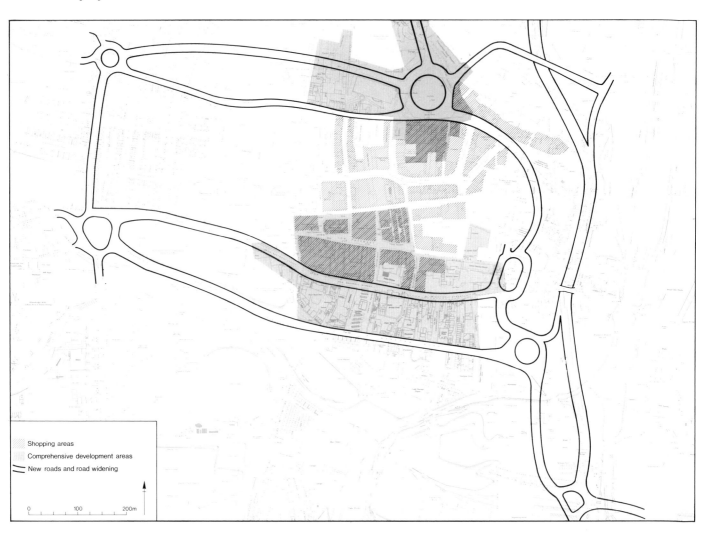

Shopping areas
Comprehensive development areas
New roads and road widening

0   100   200m

Fig 13   King and Miller Inn on north side of Market Place in 1967 prior to demolition

Fig 14   Cathedral Vaults on east side of Market Place in 1973 prior to demolition

The Civic Society argued that 'the authors of the submitted plan have written off the existing town centre as a slum ripe for redevelopment, without making a proper assessment of the character and merits of the existing arrangement. The plan seeks to erase the Market Place which has been an important element in the town for centuries.' The Derbyshire Archaeological Society likewise objected to 'the large-scale destruction of buildings of interest, especially in the Market Place area, and the erasure of the open space of the market which is a focal point in the ancient street pattern.'

At the time the man in the street, like councillors and their officials, would probably have dismissed that argument as interesting historically but irrelevant to the present day. The Civic Society came closer to touching the real psychological nerve-root when it complained that not only were historic buildings being needlessly sacrificed but the plan showed 'a lack of understanding of the aesthetic and symbolic value of buildings enduring in their original setting' (Figs 13, 14).

To the council's leadership at that time, and to the officials advising them, such arguments seemed so much high-flown, unrealistic nonsense. Chesterfield could not have its omelette without breaking eggs. Reality in the shape of economic decline stared them in the face. As the then chairman of the planning committee had put it rather earlier, 'Time is not on our side. Unless we can get ahead with this central development, we shall find that other towns around are stepping ahead, and [we are left] like a lame dog trying to catch up.'

Comprehensive redevelopment still seemed to official eyes to be Chesterfield's best means (in the words of Mr Gerard Ryan, counsel for borough and county councils) to 'bring new vigour into a decaying area.' The Inspector's report, when it was eventually published nearly three years after the inquiry closed, reflected the local authorities' view rather than the objectors'.

The Inspector, Mr Stanley Midwinter, noted that the council had sought 'the best' architectural advice; the redevelopment would be 'of good modern design on the small intimate scale' and promised 'an imaginative progression of spaces and buildings'. 'I do not,' he concluded, 'find anything in the submitted plan which would necessarily adversely affect the civic pride, sense of local identity, or self-respect engendered by the town of Chesterfield.'

But by then events and commercial reality had outstripped the planning process. Soon after the end of the inquiry Hammerson indicated to the council that they wished to withdraw from their original commitment but with the option of negotiating terms for a different development once the Minister's decision was known. The Allen plan was now seen to be over-ambitious.

A critical examination of the costs of large-scale development led by the middle of 1970 to discussions between Hammerson and the council on a markedly smaller scheme. They proposed to cut the site back on its eastern side, thus excluding The Shambles and the Central Pavement area to its south (Fig 15). They were, however, still proposing to build the new shopping centre on the Market Square, destroying the open market and demolishing the Low Pavement buildings on its southern side (Fig 16).

Fig 15   Market Place looking east, 1974

The Hammerson scheme

Hammerson's own scheme, made public in 1972 (Figs 17, 18), took the form of a single, covered megastructure, partly air-conditioned. This was to house 51 shops (20,000 sq m/215,200 sq ft) gross, an assembly hall, two public houses, and space for some of the market stalls. The majority of stalls were, however, to be transferred to New Square, which was to be left open. The Hammerson building also included parking spaces for 660 cars; there was thus no longer any need for a separate multi-storey car park in New Beetwell Street.

Although different from the Allen scheme, Hammerson's proposals were seen to be broadly in conformity with the Town Map amendments sanctioned by the Minister 11 months earlier; accordingly the CDAs and compulsory purchase orders which he had confirmed could still be the vehicle for the new scheme. Neighbouring towns – Mansfield, Alfreton, Derby, and Sheffield – all had new shopping developments under way or in preparation. This made councillors, especially the council's forceful leader Jock Anderson, and officials, led by the Town Clerk Ralph Kennedy, all the more anxious to press ahead.

35   37   39

51   53

67   69

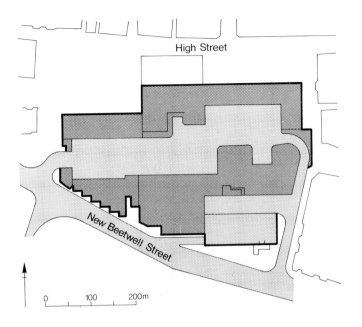

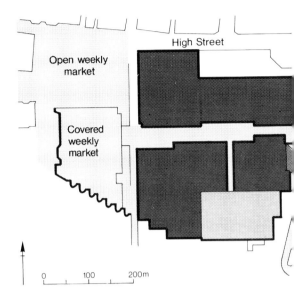

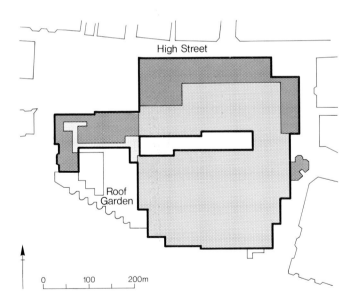

Fig 17 Scheme for a major shopping development covering Market Place, Low Pavement, and part of New Square: prepared by the Bernard Engel Partnership in 1972 for Hammerson and Chesterfield Borough Council. Service level, lower mall level, upper mall level, roof level

Fig 18 Model of the Hammerson scheme

41   43   45   47

59   61   63

71   73   75   77

0   5   10m

2 The battle for Chesterfield

If the council supposed that, with the public inquiry behind it, all would be plain sailing, then it was mistaken. With realisation of what the Hammerson development involved, disquiet had been growing. The general reaction would, nonetheless, have been to say, 'We don't like it, but we can't at this stage do anything about it.' There were, however, some citizens of Chesterfield not prepared to take 'yes' for an answer.

Counterattack

One of these was a professional engineer named Graham Robinson. He was a Chesterfield man, born and bred. Unlike the market traders, he had no commercial interest in the issue; unlike Ernest Robinson (unrelated), a Conservative Alderman on the council, he had no political allegiance. Some people claimed that he was a Tory; in fact his only political involvement had been in his teens, as a member of the Labour League of Youth. He was in the correct sense of the word *dis*interested, but very far from being *un*interested.

Robinson was moved to act by a letter published by the *Derbyshire Times* in January 1973 from David Ellis, an 11-year-old schoolboy. 'Chesterfield is a nice town – the development will spoil it,' he wrote. Robinson's first reaction was, 'We can't let this happen.' He first walked round the market checking on how the stallholders felt about the scheme. They were almost unanimous in opposing it. He then wrote a letter to the *Derbyshire Times*, asking opponents of the development to ally themselves with him.

'The time for words is past,' he wrote. 'No-one outside the political arena is coordinating the massive objection to this scheme which exists at grass-roots level. I have therefore taken it upon myself to perform that function. May I, sir, invite readers who care about the Market and are prepared to do something about it to contact me now.'

Rising tide of opposition

The letter drew many phone calls and culminated in the formation of a small *ad hoc* committee or ginger group which later named itself the Chesterfield Heritage Society. It was untiring, resourceful, well-armed with information, and – though its members did not know it at the outset – had friends in high and strategic places.

What is more, time and the tide of public opinion were with it. In retrospect, its success can be seen as that of a well-organised delaying action. But this was a delaying action stubbornly and ingeniously sustained over two years, and it gained additional strength from being able to propose a positive alternative to what it was fighting.

Its first action was to mount a petition against the Hammerson scheme. Robinson and his colleagues had little experience of how to organise this, but from the first wet and windy hour of collecting

Fig 19   No 41 Low Pavement in 1973, one of a listed building group threatened with demolition

Fig 20   No 43 Low Pavement in 1973, listed but threatened

signatures, it was clear that Chesterfield was behind them. They felt that almost electric atmosphere known to political canvassers for whose party the tide is running strongly, when smiles and encouraging words replace the usual noncommittal response.

Market traders

In the market the council's own agent, the market superintendent, demanded that traders take down the pro-petition posters from their stalls. In theory they faced eviction if they ignored this instruction. Robinson cannily urged them to comply. If the posters went up again when the superintendent's back was turned, that was another matter. He couldn't be everywhere at once.

The superintendent's efforts were, of course, counter-productive. They left the traders more unified and determined than ever in their opposition. Robinson himself was encouraged when the manager of Boots the Chemists, then on the corner of High Street and Glumangate, emerged not to complain but to offer to lower his shop awning to give some protection from the rain. The petition eventually drew more than 32,000 signatures, the bulk of them from people living or regularly shopping in Chesterfield; and though, predictably, councillors in favour of the development sought to argue the unreliability of petitions as a means of gauging people's considered and serious opinions, a petition of this size – something like half the population of Chesterfield – could not easily be laughed off. The size of the protest was a tremendous fillip for the campaign; but it was also, most of those concerned now recognise, one of the main reasons why the council eventually changed its policy.

Meanwhile, however, like a great ocean-going tanker incapable of stopping for some miles after the signal has been given to reverse, the borough council continued to prepare for the redevelopment. The then Town Clerk, Ralph Kennedy, was utterly committed to the scheme as in the best interests of Chesterfield; he had little time for conservation arguments.

Jennifer Jenkins takes an interest

Mrs (now Dame) Jennifer Jenkins discovered that in no uncertain fashion. She had a personal concern for Chesterfield: her father, Parker Morris, was one of Kennedy's predecessors as Town Clerk before going on to Westminster City Council and the report on public housing standards which made his name famous. Mrs Jenkins remembered the Market Place well from her childhood. When the strength of public feeling against the Hammerson scheme reached the national headlines, she was secretary of the Ancient Monuments Society, one of the national amenity societies soon to be charged by statute with commenting on proposals to demolish or alter listed buildings.

She therefore wrote a conciliatory letter to Ralph Kennedy offering to mediate between the council and the objectors. His letter in reply was 'the curtest brush-off I have ever had in my life.' It made her determined to do her best to save the Market Place. And two years later she was to become Chairman of the Historic Buildings Council.

Fig 21 Nos 41 and 43 Low Pavement in 1973. Rear view showing Castle Yard

Consent to demolish

The council's next step was to submit to Derbyshire County Council an outline planning application for the Hammerson scheme. Despite such fierce opposition the county approved this conditionally in May 1973. For the permission to be effective, the borough council needed to obtain listed building consent to demolish four listed buildings; three were on Low Pavement on the south side of the Market Place (Figs 19–24) while the fourth, a Quakers' Meeting House north of Saltergate, stood in the way of a proposed multi-storey car park. The application to demolish was considered at a further public inquiry in August 1973 and approved by the Minister, on the advice of his Inspector, in November 1973.

In retrospect that decision may seem remarkable. But when one looks at the circumstances and climate of opinion then prevailing, it is understandable. On the one hand, the Department of the Environment and its predecessor Ministry had, after an extensive enquiry, backed comprehensive development. Listing an historic building does not guarantee its preservation and never has done so. It simply requires that any proposal to destroy or seriously alter it is carefully considered in the light of preservation policy. Its quality and importance as an historic building have to be weighed against other factors such as any benefit to the community from redevelopment, for instance by bringing new life and investment to a run-down area.

To be consistent with their past approvals, Ministers and their advisers were bound to weigh the advantages of redevelopment heavily in the scales. Moreover, at that time, the standards applied to

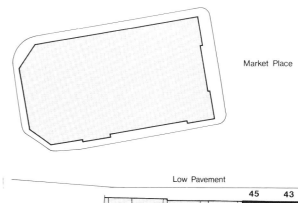

Market Place

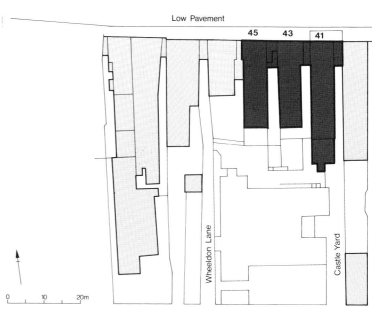

Low Pavement

Wheeldon Lane

Castle Yard

Fig 22 Nos 41, 43, and 45 Low Pavement, a listed building group showing adjoining buildings and passageways

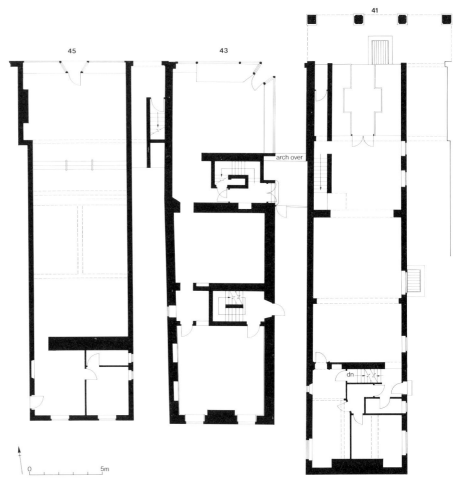

**Fig 23 Nos 41, 43, and 45 Low Pavement.
Ground and first floor**

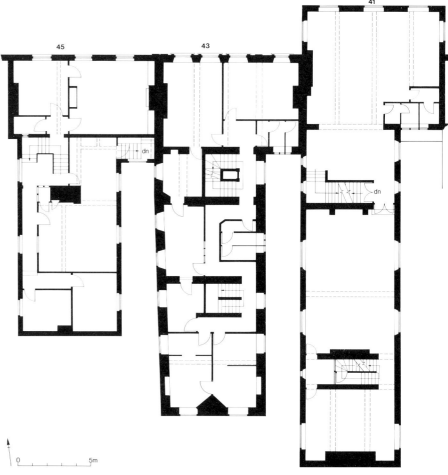

Fig 24 Nos 41, 43, and 45 Low Pavement. Elevation

judgement of quality in listed buildings were very much more conservative and restrictive than they are today. Once it had listed building consent, the borough council was able to obtain detailed planning permission for the scheme.

But there followed a series of events that were to jolt and finally sap the council's determination.

Peacock fire sheds light on history

In February 1974 a public house called the Peacock, at the New Square end of the Low Pavement range of buildings, had caught fire. Local historians had long suspected that the down-at-heel Victorian frontage hid a much older building; the fire, which did relatively little damage to the historic timber frame, revealed enough of what was behind to make it plain that this was a timber-framed building of outstanding interest (Figs 25–28).

Fig 25 Peacock Inn, Low Pavement, 1974

There had followed a ding-dong correspondence between the Heritage Society and the Department of the Environment's historic buildings section which would have caused anyone less determined to give up in despair. It went rather as follows.

A circular argument

CHS: 'This building is much older and more important than we thought. Please list it.'

DoE: 'Our experts advise that, though it may be old, the building has been so overlaid by alteration as not to be listable.'

CHS: 'We attach an expert report showing that it is substantially all there and can be restored. The building is a unique survival in this part of Derbyshire. Come and look.'

DoE: 'Our experts have not visited the site, but are trained to assess buildings to the standards laid down and have looked at the material you sent. They consider the building should not be listed.'

A bad press

By this time, however (March 1974), the council was getting a very bad press not only in local papers like the *Sheffield Star*, but in the *Sunday Times* (Ian Nairn), the *Observer* (Christopher Booker and Bennie Gray), and *The Architects' Journal*. So was the Department of the Environment for its refusal to list the Peacock. Each organisation preserved a united front, but in fact each had its doubters, arguing in private against what they felt they had to defend in public.

A writ is served

Chesterfield Heritage Society now decided to resort to shock tactics. Sensing that the handover on 1 April 1974 from the old borough council to a new and larger authority with wider powers might be the signal for an irrevocable start on the scheme, it chose that day to serve a writ on the council.

It was taken out in the names of three leading members of the society, all Chesterfield ratepayers: Graham Robinson, Bill Kennerley, and Roy Davidson, a cheese factor with a stall in the market as well as a shop nearby. It claimed that 'the agreement proposed to be entered into between the Defendant and the Hammerson Group of Companies . . . would give rise to a loss or deficiency on the accounts of the defendant which would be surchargeable under Section 228 (1) (d) of the Local Government Act 1933 and/or Section 161 (49) (b) of the Local Government Act 1972.'

That writ, it is now conceded, was a colossal piece of bluff. But it served its purpose. Shock waves ran through the Town Hall and councillors supporting the development. The threat of personal

Fig 26 Peacock Inn *c* 1800 showing setting with adjoining 'burgage' plots

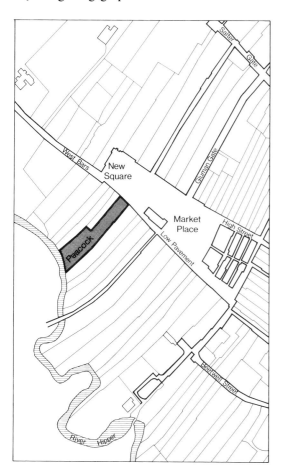

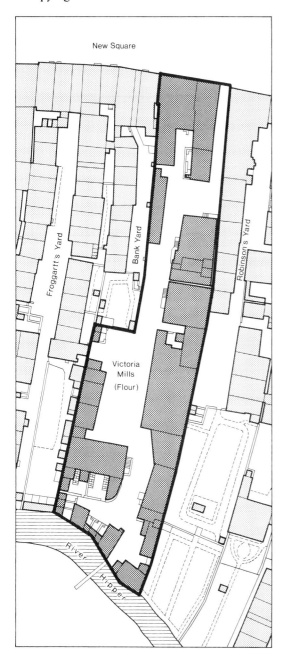

Fig 27   Peacock Inn _c_ 1880 showing a flour mill occupying land to the rear

surcharge, even if you are assured it is unlikely to succeed, is calculated to make most councillors think again quite carefully about what they are doing. And until the matter had been resolved, in court or by out of court agreement, there could be no question of the council signing any agreement.

Hammerson withdraws

A very few days later came a third hammer blow. Hammerson withdrew. A downturn in the property market generally and the First Lettings Tax announced by Chancellor of the Exchequer, Anthony Barber, in his 1974 Budget – a measure the cost of which developers found difficult to predict – had considerably cooled their enthusiasm for the Chesterfield project. The writ was probably the last straw. The game was no longer worth the candle.

Fig 28   Peacock Inn. The timber frame

'. . . Quite imprudent. . .'

'In the circumstances, therefore, it is considered quite imprudent, indeed irresponsible, to embark on the town centre proposals until it is possible to assess accurately the impact of the new fiscal regulations.' Although in principle the withdrawal was temporary, the terms of the company statement certainly did not encourage anyone to hope that the scheme would be quickly resurrected.

23

3 Looking for a way out

On the face of it, the council sought to give the impression that it would still press on with a clear-and-rebuild scheme. Even the spot-listing in August 1974 of the Peacock (a DoE historic buildings inspector had eventually come and been persuaded that the building was 'of listable quality') did not alter the resolve of Town Clerk Ralph Kennedy.

Dismantle the Peacock?

On the one hand, both the council and the DoE stressed that listing did not guarantee preservation. On the other hand, however, the process of weighing up the pros and cons could be lengthy, probably involving a public inquiry. That is why, in order to push ahead its development, Ralph Kennedy began canvassing the acceptability of dismantling and re-erecting the Peacock. In purely physical terms, this would not have been difficult with a timber-framed building.

But it soon became plain that the weight of objections would be considerable. Those opposed included not only the defenders of the Market Place but the Society for the Protection of Ancient Buildings – the national society consulted by the government on historic buildings of this kind and age. And the SPAB has always as a matter of principle opposed the moving of historic buildings from their original sites.

New development proposals

So in April 1975 the council invited two new organisations to put forward proposals: Enterprise Developments of Chesterfield Ltd, formed by a group of local businessmen, and Bernard Engel & Partners, consultant architects retained by the council itself. In addition, Sheffield estate agents Eadon Lockwood & Riddle took the initiative in putting forward a third proposal in sketch form. Significantly the brief drawn up by the council asked BEP and Enterprise Developments 'to give consideration to the possibility of conserving the whole or part of the existing Market Place and of conserving certain listed buildings within the area. . .'.

Another significant change was that development should be capable of being phased 'so as to provide economic units of development over a period of years.' For the first time the borough council was publicly accepting the possibility of (a) a conservation-geared redevelopment and (b) an incremental as opposed to a 'one big bang' approach to redevelopment.

DoE reserve powers

At this stage, too, the Department of the Environment and the Historic Buildings Council began to show their hand. The Town and Country

Amenities Act, passed in August 1974, gave the Secretary of State for the Environment the power – previously confined to local authorities – himself to designate conservation areas. This was a reserve power which it was always envisaged he would use only in exceptional circumstances. In that same month Brian Hennessy, an architect-planner from the DoE's Historic Areas Division headed by Philip Waddington, had made a survey of Chesterfield with a view to the possible designation of a conservation area.

So was the Chesterfield situation exceptional? The Heritage Society were in no doubt that it was; inside the DoE they were not so sure. Reluctance to intervene rested on at least two trenchant objections: the department would be undermining a redevelopment it had, on the basis of more than one public inquiry, broadly approved; and the affair would not end with designation.

The DoE would need, logically, to fulfil the follow-up duties of investigating and deciding all applications for demolition (unlisted buildings in a conservation area became, under the 1974 Town and Country Amenities Act, subject to demolition control); it would also, arguably, by stepping into the shoes of the local authority, acquire a duty to promote the area's (much needed) enhancement.

These were responsibilities DoE officers had no wish to undertake from afar, quite possibly in the face of local authority hostility. Nonetheless the assumed threat of designation did play its part in the council's willingness in April 1975 to consider fresh options, as described above. In addition, the chairman of the Planning Committee had given an undertaking, a month after Hennessy's survey, not to demolish until redevelopment was imminent.

Economic climate changes

The situation had altered. A changing economic climate made the original scale of development seem at least questionable, and the council itself was canvassing the possibility of a degree of conservation. In September 1975 Hennessy went back to update his survey, this time with the assistance of an experienced and sympathetic valuer from the DoE's East Midlands regional office.

The valuer's contribution was to demonstrate that the figures for shopping demand which had formed the basis of the Hammerson scheme were over-optimstic. They derived from an economically more buoyant period than the mid 1970s.

New attitudes to 'heritage'

The two-year build-up to European Architectural Heritage Year, 1975, had also helped to change the climate of official opinion, by making conservation a subject of more widespread interest than it had previously been, and by promoting the message that it was not limited to 'five-star' towns like York and Bath. Every town and village, no matter how humble, had something worth conserving – had in fact an 'architectural heritage'.

Personalities were also important. Council leader Jock Anderson, who was absolutely determined to give Chesterfield a new and modern centre and saw little of value in the market place area, had been followed in that post first by Councillor John Ford and then by a man on whom, as the Planning Committee chairman, defence of the redevelopment scheme had largely devolved: Bill Flanagan.

In 1974 Jock Anderson died. Councillor Flanagan had for some time had his doubts about the clean sweep approach; opinion within the ruling Labour group had also softened and become more fluid, at least partly as a result of the 1973 petition and the widespread opposition it represented.

The borough planning officer, Tom Knuckey, had appeared committed to the development, having before local government reorganisation worked on the planning framework for it. His commitment, however, appears to have been to a large-scale shopping redevelopment and only incidentally to redevelopment on the Market Place as the best means to that end. In 1975 Mr Knuckey too died and was succeeded that autumn by his senior group leader, Michael Kennedy, who favoured a conservation approach.

A 'respectable' way out

So when the DoE, encouraged and prodded by Mrs Jenkins as the HBC's new chairman, offered a respectable way out, Flanagan – and, after some hesitation, the majority of the key Policy Committee – accepted it. The proposal was that the DoE and the council should jointly appoint (and jointly pay for) consultants to investigate whether a viable and attractive shopping redevelopment and the conservation approach could be made to work together.

This was approved in September 1975 by Chesterfield's Policy Committee and in October by the full council. On 27 November a joint DoE/borough meeting was convened to select a short-list of architects to undertake the reappraisal.

Choosing consultants

They chose three firms without too much difficulty: Gordon Benoy & Partners, who had designed a very successful shopping scheme behind the facades of the market place at Newark-on-Trent; Building Design Partnership, a large practice with much experience of shopping but also considered to have a sympathetic approach to existing townscape; and – at the other end of the spectrum – Gordon Michell & Partners, a small practice which had carried out exemplary conservation and infill work in a number of towns, notably Cirencester.

There was some debate as to whether to include a fourth name, and if so which. Eventually the committee agreed to add Feilden & Mawson, a Norwich-based practice with excellent conservation credentials but little experience of designing shopping centres.

The final selection was made on 15 December by a selection panel which included borough, county, and DoE officers and Chesterfield councillors. Dr Bernard Feilden, then senior partner of the Feilden & Mawson practice, by all accounts took the meeting by storm. He appealed particularly to elected members by his enthusiasm for Chesterfield and its conservation potential, as well as by a robust and well-argued case for retaining more than just the facades of market place buildings. A vote produced a decisive majority for his firm.

Quick off the mark

Having taken the plunge, Chesterfield could not start soon enough. The deputy Town Clerk, Denis Harrison, wrote the next morning offering Feilden the job, pausing only after the letter had gone off to phone the DoE for their detailed agreement. Harrison's sense of urgency probably reflected not only his own enthusiasm for a conservation outcome but the keenness of Councillor Flanagan and his fellow members to 'get the study on the road' immediately after Christmas.

The DoE representative at the selection meeting, Philip Waddington, remarked after the 15 December meeting that most of Chesterfield's elected members now seemed 'ready to receive a solution very different from the previous schemes which were [to be] built over so much of the market square.' The next step would be to demonstrate that such a 'very different solution' could be made to work.

Feilden, with 25 years' experience of working in the Civic Amenity Movement, which included the Civic Trust Norwich Magdalen Street scheme (1957) and research for Sir Colin Buchanan's Traffic in Towns (1962), realised that Chesterfield Town Council would most readily appreciate the economic arguments for conservation. He therefore began a systematic condition survey of all the properties on Low Pavement. By doing so he also hoped to integrate a full understanding of their historical values and physical condition into the project design.

On completing the survey he advised the Town Council that the properties on Low Pavement could be rehabilitated for two-thirds of the cost of new buildings of an equal area with the exception of the Peacock Inn, which might cost three times as much as new building because of its archaeological value.

4　Putting together a package

The machinery for the Chesterfield Central Area Study consisted of two tiers: a Steering Group representing the 'client' organisations and consisting of borough and county councillors and a senior representative of the DoE, and a Working Party which reported to it.

Conservation 'a must'

The Working Party's remit was 'with the least possible delay to reach agreement with the Department of the Environment and Derbyshire County Council upon the form of a redevelopment of CDA1 which best reconciles the urgent need for new and efficient shopping facilities with the desirability of conserving those buildings and features which are of historic or architectural interest.' At the same time it would make proposals for the remainder of the town centre – in effect the whole of Chesterfield as it had developed by the mid nineteenth century.

The difference between the two approaches is significant. Anyone drawing up a CDA will want, for legal and commercial reasons, to limit the area to be put forward for approval in order to simplify negotiations with landowners and minimise public inquiry objections and acquisition costs. Conservation objectives can and should be directed at a broader target. In order to reinforce a town's existing identity and character, they look for as much retention, repair, and reuse of existing buildings as possible.

The main objectives

But conservation in Chesterfield had to be reconciled with commercial and social objectives, as the council's brief spelled out. It detailed three main objectives:

1   Identify the economic and social need for new shopping development. Method: take figures produced by the local authorities and their consultants and update them as much as possible in the light of later information.

2   Identify opportunities for conservation and enhancement. Method: identify areas, buildings, features of intrinsic merit; assess their individual and group value, present and potential use, physical condition and problems/costs of adaptation, improvement, and repair.

3   Identify opportunities for development. Method: look not just at shopping, but also at ancillary requirements such as parking and servicing. Investigate the scope for new building and for keeping and reusing existing buildings. Look at present shopping patterns, and pedestrian and vehicle flows as they affect the shopping potential of different parts of the study area.

The Working Party

On the Working Party the borough council was represented by the Town Clerk (in practice invariably represented by his deputy, Denis Harrison), the chief planning and estates officer, Michael Kennedy, and their colleagues, the chief technical services, financial, and environmental health officers, plus the transport manager (the borough runs local bus services).

Derbyshire County Council's representative was the county planning officer, Harry Cowley, often represented by an historic buildings architect, Derek Latham.

The Department of the Environment was represented by the head of its Historic Areas Conservation Division, Philip Waddington, and the Senior Estates Officer from its East Midlands Region.

Bernard Feilden led the Chesterfield team until his firm's scheme was approved. Then, on his appointment as Director of the

International Centre for the Study of Preservation and Restoration of Cultural Property in Rome, he handed over to his partner, Geoff Mitchell, who had been involved since the conception of the project. They were assisted by architect planner Maldwyn Morgan, development architect Simon Crosse, and landscape architect Rosamunde Reich of Feilden & Mawson's Norwich office.

Other consultants were called on as needed, notably chartered surveyors Goddard & Smith and quantity surveyors Summers & Partners. The borough engineer's department supplied traffic management expertise. Tony Smith of Goddard & Smith worked particularly closely with Geoffrey Mitchell in the months which followed – months which were to prove critical to the eventual outcome.

Feilden & Mawson's remit

Feilden & Mawson as architectural planning consultants were primarily concerned with objectives 2 and 3. Within this remit, their detailed terms of reference covered nine specific points. They were to:

1 Identify areas/properties/features intrinsically worthy of retention and enhancement.

2 Draw up an outline programme of enhancement, including new infill where necessary, these proposals to be feasible economically.

3 Assess individual properties for their individual and group value, existing and potential use, physical condition, and problems of adaptation, improvement, and repair.

4 Comment on properties blighted by road and redevelopment proposals.

5 Identify areas (for instance cleared sites, blighted areas of little significance, sites severed by new roads) which require redevelopment; suggest how such redevelopment can best be dovetailed into the existing town structure in terms of function, accessibility, and architectural form.

6 Indicate possible servicing and pedestrianisation arrangements.

7 Advise on the townscape/conservation implications of the three current shopping redevelopment schemes for CDA1.

8 If necessary, devise in broad sketch terms a new scheme or schemes for development and enhancement.

9 Suggest what area or areas warrant conservation area designation.

Independent advice

The key point of this briefing was paragraph 8. Despite the 'if necessary', this provided clear authorisation to Feilden & Mawson to demonstrate the feasibility and attractiveness of a conservation approach. F & M's Geoff Mitchell also pinpoints another key feature of the commission to his firm: their advice was to be independent and, in a sense, sacrosanct. They were to operate within the framework of the Working Party, but the Working Party was expressly forbidden to alter their report.

In fact, says Mitchell, the Working Party and the consultants quickly settled down into a positive and amicable working relationship. Feilden & Mawson never needed to stress their independent position within it. The group worked by frequent and informal exchange of ideas and information, with formal presentations kept to the minimum. This made for speed as well as flexibility. But it may be that the presence of that formal independence was salutary. Everyone knew they had it, and so no-one – even supposing they had wanted to – was disposed to challenge it. And the fact that their independence was guaranteed must undoubtedly have strengthened the consultants' position.

Who costs the conservation element?

Another important clarification emerged from the December 1975 meeting of the Working Party. It concerned conservation costings, which are a difficult and controversial subject. Many a conservation scheme has sunk without trace because costings were produced by quantity surveyors either not expert in this field or unsympathetic to conservation objectives. The costs of repair and adaptation necessarily contain large areas of uncertainty; those for clear-and-rebuild appear clear-cut. When the two are in competition, the tendency is for the apparently quantifiable to win over the notoriously unquantifiable.

In the event, no conflict arose. When Bernard Feilden reported that, in his opinion, the buildings in Low Pavement could be rehabilitated for two-thirds of the cost of new construction, the Town Clerk instructed his architect's department to work out two schemes which were costed by the Corporation's own consultant quantity surveyors. The result confirmed Feilden's opinion. This was vital to reassure the Council that conservation need not be more costly than new building work.

Show that it's feasible!

The position now was that Chesterfield Council was willing to entertain a conservation-based solution to its shopping needs, but had to be convinced that this would work. In a sense the onus was on the Working Party and the council's consultants to demonstrate its feasibility; but if and when they did demonstrate it to the satisfaction of the steering group, most councillors and leading officials were now ready to accept that approach.

The council was not at this stage formally rejecting or jettisoning existing schemes – two prepared for it by consultant architects Bernard Engel & Partners and one put forward by Enterprise Developments on behalf of a group of Chesterfield traders. But if these schemes were found wanting against a conservation yardstick, then Feilden & Mawson were authorised to produce something better.

Setting the pace

The pace had been set by Councillor Bill Flanagan and Deputy Town Clerk Denis Harrison. The Working Party, chaired by Harrison, kept up the impetus. It met for the first time just eight days after the consultants had been appointed – on the eve of Christmas Eve 1975. It agreed to set up three sub-groups – commercial, traffic, and conservation – and handed out tasks to each. The Feilden & Mawson team departed for Christmas knowing that they had to produce their first results by the end of January. The target for the Working Party's report was the end of March 1976. In the event it did well to deliver its final report in May of that year.

Three sub-groups

The three sub-groups were made up as follows:

Commercial development: borough planning officer, deputy Town Clerk, assistant county planner, DoE regional office valuer, and economic consultants Goddard & Smith

Traffic: borough technical services officer, borough planning officer, and borough transport manager (assistant county planner and DoE representative available if required)

Conservation: borough planning officer, DoE Historic Areas representative, assistant county planning officer, and planning and architectural consultants Feilden & Mawson

This last group (comprising borough planning and estates officer Michael Kennedy, Derek Latham representing Derbyshire County Council, and Philip Waddington, head of DoE Historic Areas Division) may be rightly regarded as 'pro-conservation', but each answered to masters who required them to be sure that the commercial and social objectives of redevelopment could really be achieved through a conservation solution. This was certainly the position of borough planner Michael Kennedy. He, as a member of all three sub-groups, also played a key role as link man.

The task of the Commercial sub-group was essentially to establish what level and type of shopping development the town now needed and could support.

The Conservation sub-group needed first to demonstrate the architectural townscape value of buildings which had been undervalued and in many cases allowed to deteriorate in anticipation of redevelopment; to appraise existing redevelopment schemes; and, if these appeared unacceptable, to consider an alternative scheme (drawn up by Feilden & Mawson) showing how retention and refurbishment of such buildings could go hand in hand with the required shopping provision.

The Traffic sub-group had to demonstrate ways in which a conservation-based development could be made to work for the purposes of servicing, car parking, and vehicular and pedestrian circulation. It started from the premise that the town centre should have a sizeable traffic-free or pedestrian priority zone.

Conservation, not preservation

Feilden & Mawson's most urgent task was to survey the Chesterfield townscape and assess the quality of buildings and spaces. Its approach pinpoints the difference between preservation and conservation. Chesterfield, the consultants readily conceded, 'is not a town packed with historic monuments and buildings of national importance, but it does possess an unusually high proportion of good buildings which together make valuable townscape.'

Among the qualities they identified were use of local materials and the effect of weathering on those materials; the 'grain' of the town, with a series of interesting streets and alleyways creating 'a vigorous street character with a friendly human scale, reinforced by surviving medieval plot widths'; the two green areas around church and Town Hall, at either end of the main east–west axis; and the way in which views out into open country alternate with places of tight enclosure, creating 'drama and surprising contrasts'.

These and other positive qualities of the town the Feilden & Mawson team both analysed and demonstrated to the study group with slides and drawings. A sentence from their research report for the DoE, though modestly understated, says it all: '. . . the Working Party concluded that, for the most part, Chesterfield town centre possessed a wider range of features worthy of retention and enhancement than had previously been identified.'

'Missing teeth'

But Chesterfield also had its weaknesses. The F & M analysis pinpointed in particular the 'missing teeth' in its agreeable countenance: gap sites which destroyed the unity of its townscape and by their scruffiness devalued the town's appeal, commercially as well as visually. Some were used as car parks, but because the use was regarded as temporary, remained scruffy. These were sites for which development was thought to be imminent; but in Chesterfield, as in other towns facing ambitious but difficult-to-achieve redevelopment schemes, that imminence had receded and receded.

Some visually important sites were empty because no firm plans existed for any permanent use. One good example was the large traffic island at the junction of Holywell Cross and Saltergate, used as a temporary car park. Its history was that the planning authority had originally allocated it for a new telephone exchange. This would have been an inadequate presence for so prominent a site, and the council negotiated a land swap with what was then Post Office Telecommunications. This preserved the site for a more appropriate use, but did nothing for it visually in the short term. What should have terminated a vista was instead a vacuum; where urban space should have been defined and contained, it leaked dismally out of the town.

The consultants also identified another townscape weakness on the council's own doorstep. The Town Hall (1930s *beaux arts*, topping a rise some 200m north-west of the Market Place) is, they said, a fine building, but 'stands in an open and unfriendly setting flanked by large car parks.' Hostile in bad weather and always somewhat forbidding to the pedestrian, this desert of surrounding plateau needed new buildings and planting to soften, protect, and enclose it. The effect of this could also be to reinforce its impressive *beaux arts* vista downhill towards the nineteenth-century Queens Park.

Steering development

The consultants' and the Working Party's approach to mending the townscape was to steer development to achieve this objective, as and when it occurred or could be persuaded to occur. Shopping redevelopment could be used in the short term to achieve this mending in the Low Pavement/Market Place area. Everyone realised that the wider process would necessarily be gradual and incremental. We shall see later the places where townscape repair has been achieved and where it remains to be tackled.

From this analysis of listed buildings, townscape, and spaces sprang the shortest section in the Working Party's 120 page report – the map and two pages offering recommendations for designation of a conservation area. This town centre conservation area, formally designated in June 1976, not only gave the council control over demolition of unlisted buildings but also more leverage on the design quality of planning applications (see Fig 31).

Positive enhancement

The Working Party stressed the council's duty, following designation, to promote positive enhancement. It hoped that both borough and county councils would 'allocate regular finance – even in these difficult times – to commence and sustain a steady programme of improvement work.' Such a programme, with paving and planting playing a key role, could take advantage of DoE grants. It would in the long term be 'money well spent as the town becomes increasingly attractive to both shoppers and holiday makers'.

At the same time as the Conservation sub-group was examining the strengths and weaknesses of Chesterfield's townscape, its Commercial counterpart was looking at shopping need and potential, with Tony Smith of consultant surveyors and shopping specialists Goddard & Smith taking a leading role. The study team found that no shopping development had been undertaken in the town for a decade, and that Chesterfield had lost ground not only to big cities like Sheffield and Nottingham but to smaller centres which had redeveloped such as Mansfield, Sutton, and Worksop.

How much shopping is needed?

In order to pin down the shopping requirement realistically, it was decided to carry out a new survey of retail floor space and demand. This was undertaken by Chesterfield and Derbyshire planners with Goddard & Smith and the DoE regional office. They used a computer technique which builds on three key factors: increase in catchment area

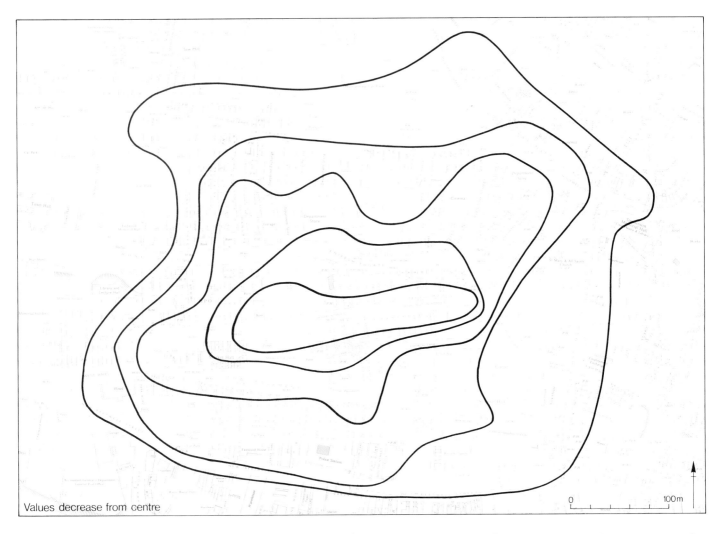

Values decrease from centre

0   100m

Fig 29 Information prepared by Goddard & Smith, consultants to the Borough Council. Relative shopping values

population; increase in spending power and changes in spending patterns; and relative attractiveness as against other centres.

They found that catchment area population, though it had increased and was still increasing, was now predicted to grow more slowly than earlier estimates.

Increases in spending were admitted to be difficult to predict, and the team noted that the previously rapid rise in spending on durable goods had slowed down between 1971 and 1976. It was not now expected to rise at all rapidly. They therefore adopted conservative growth estimates of 0.5% per annum for convenience goods and 1.75% for durables, giving an overall growth of 1.18% per annum. This compared with 1.91% suggested by the National Economic Development Office (NEDO) in 1971.

The study group measured the attractiveness of the centre by looking at its turnover and accessibility (in road travel time) from places within the catchment area.

An extra 16,000 sq m

From all this emerged the prediction that Chesterfield turnover should grow from £16.2m in 1971 to £24.2m in real terms by 1986. This £24.2m comprised £5.7m convenience goods and £18.4m durable goods. After making allowance for existing traders increasing their turnover and for retail planning consents already given, the team

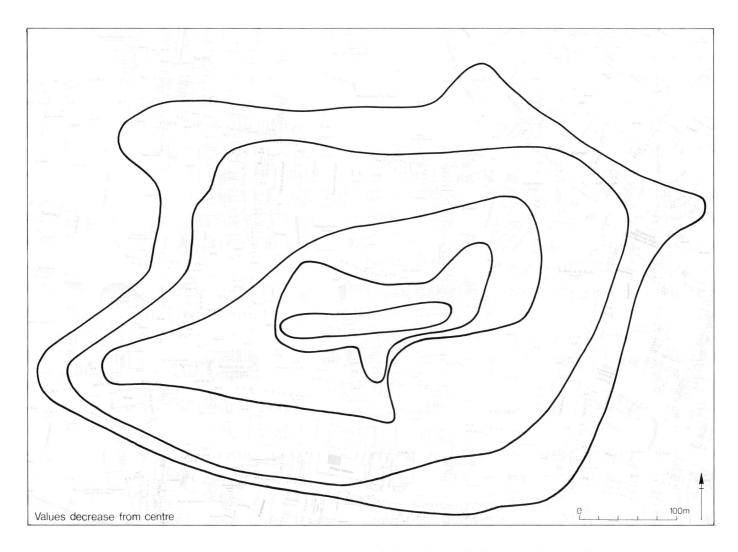

Values decrease from centre

0   100m

Fig 30 Information prepared by Goddard & Smith, consultants to the Borough Council. Shop rents

estimated that Chesterfield required an additional 16,200 sq m, 175,000 sq ft, of shopping floor space (retail and storage). This was the net increase, excluding replacement of any shops demolished prior to redevelopment.

They then looked at other uses such as offices and housing. The state of the office market in 1976 dictated that an office ingredient must be limited to small suites in existing buildings; housing might fulfil a demand, but team members were conscious of difficulties about combining homes with shops in new developments, and postponed any final view on this until the design of the refurbished Low Pavement building became clearer. In the event, this space was used for offices.

Market and 'risk foods'

What of Chesterfield's markets, a feature of the town since medieval times? Both open and covered markets undoubtedly drew people to the town; but both had suffered from redevelopment delays. The open market did not meet some food hygiene requirements; the market hall lacked some required facilities. The best way forward seemed to be to transfer 'risk foods' to a new or upgraded market hall and provide extra facilities for the open market. The team established a need for some 220 stalls in the open air and about 70 indoors.

So what the study was now looking at was ways of providing upwards of 16,000 sq m of new shopping while at the same time conserving, repairing, and enhancing all that was most attractive in the town centre. But in order to achieve that new shopping, Chesterfield council needed capital from either a developer or a funding institution like a pension fund or insurance company. And such bodies are by habit commercially conservative: they generally want to develop in or very close to the 'prime' shopping pitch, typically where such leading multiples as Marks & Spencer and Boots are already operating.

The prime pitch

In Chesterfield in 1976 this prime pitch ran, as High Street, along the north side of the Market Place and out of it along the north side of The Shambles, then on into Burlington Street (Figs 29, 30). Most developers or institutions would want to be on or as close to that as possible. That was what had led to the Allen and Hammerson proposals to build over the Market Place. By contrast, from a conservation point of view, the best – and perhaps only acceptable – place to fit in 16,000 sq m of new shopping was on the sloping, partly cleared backlands area behind Low Pavement.

5 Changing people's perceptions

On a map, the distance from the High Street pavement across the Market Place to the Low Pavement backlands may not look much. It is less than 100m. But, as Michael Kennedy recalls, to at least one hard-headed property man on a wet and windy day, and with Low Pavement properties looking down-at heel and unappealing, the distance was quite unacceptable.

New magnets, new desire lines

So the consultants, who were by this time at work on producing their 'conservation alternative' to existing proposals, found themselves seeking ways of changing people's perceptions of distance and direction, by creating new magnets, new routes, and new desire lines.

The bus station south of this Pavements development area exerted only a moderate pull. To reinforce it they proposed something much more powerful: a large multi-storey car park opening on to the main town centre distributor road. A sizeable proportion of its car spaces would be on a level with F & M's main shopping mall, connected to it by an enclosed pedestrian bridge across New Beetwell Street.

This mall, 100m long, would run east–west and be built behind the retained Low Pavement buildings. It would in turn connect by a series of entrance malls, echoing the old lanes and alleys. The new shopping development thus stood athwart a main pedestrian route from car parks and buses to Market Place and High Street (Fig 31).

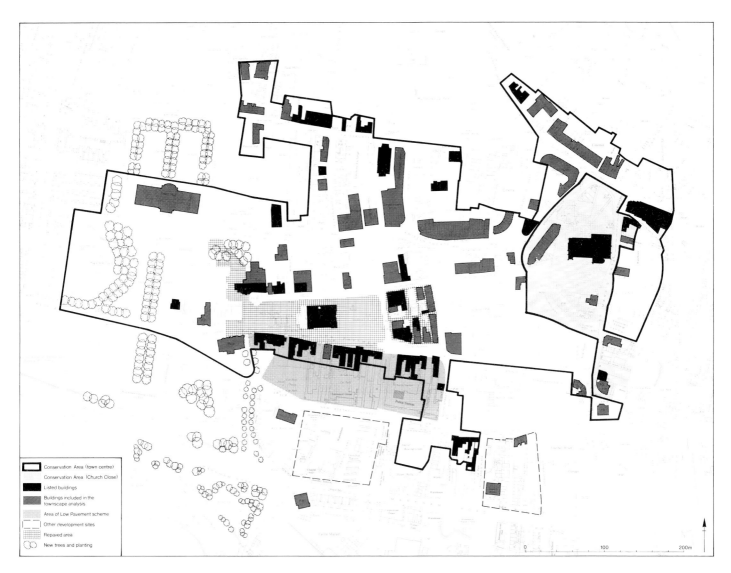

Conservation Area (town centre)
Conservation Area (Church Close)
Listed buildings
Buildings included in the townscape analysis
Area of Low Pavement scheme
Other development sites
Repaved area
New trees and planting

Fig 31 Proposals for conserving the town centre prepared in 1976 by Feilden & Mawson, architectural consultants to the Borough Council

A well-balanced centre

But a shopping development itself requires its own magnets. A well-balanced, attractive shopping centre needs shops of a variety of kinds and sizes. It needs a supermarket or supermarkets for convenience purchases and a 'variety store' selling a wide range of consumer durables. These 'anchor tenants' may have to be signed up early, usually at lower rentals per sq ft, in order to demonstrate viability.

Around and between them the developer seeks to create a varied and profitable tenant mix, and generally speaking he prefers to postpone firm lettings so that actual construction and the imminence of trading enable him to ask higher rentals. The smaller tenants tend to provide atmosphere and drawing power to a town centre scheme, and also a large proportion of the rental income.

Low-cost servicing

The Working Party in its report argued that the council should not try to cram too much on to the Low Pavement site. There were several reasons for this. First, a single level mall without air-conditioning

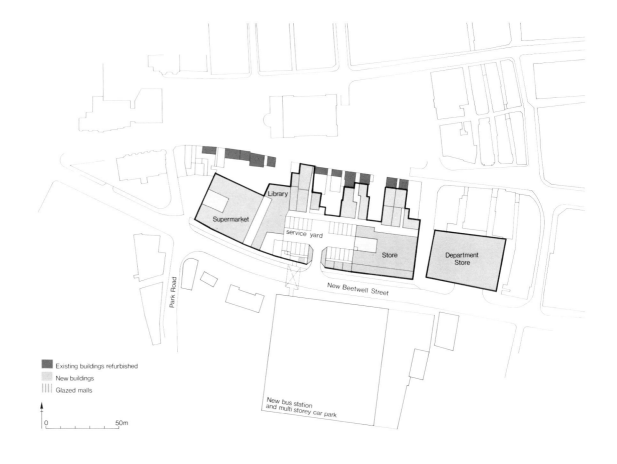

Existing buildings refurbished
New buildings
|||| Glazed malls

0   50m

Park Road

Library

Supermarket

service yard

Store

Department Store

New Beetwell Street

New bus station and multi storey car park

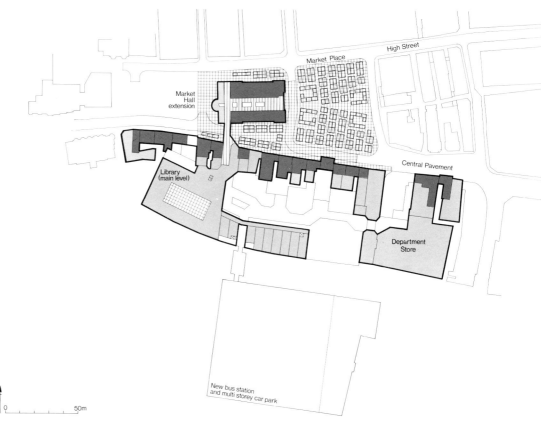

High Street

Market Place

Market Hall extension

Library (main level)

Central Pavement

Department Store

New bus station and multi storey car park

0   50m

Fig 32   Scheme for a major shopping development incorporating the existing Low Pavement frontage and Market Hall prepared in 1976 by Feilden & Mawson for the Borough Council. Service level and mall level

Fig 33   Feilden & Mawson scheme. Market Hall extension

Fig 34   Feilden & Mawson scheme. Upper floor in a restored Market Hall

would be cheaper both to build and to run. A more ambitious scheme with two or more retail levels could require air conditioning, and would be more difficult and expensive to manage and maintain. Potential tenants who had faced spiralling service charges elsewhere might be chary of involvement.

By contrast, the F & M scheme (Figs 32–36) proposed a single-level mall connecting to its south with buses and new car park and to its north with Market Place and Market Hall. Servicing was to be tucked in beneath it using the fall of the site down to New Beetwell Street to provide lorry access. Informal soundings with potential tenants, including a supermarket operator, suggested that this relatively modest, clear-cut solution would commend itself to the trade.

Spreading the benefits

Secondly, the Working Party argued, too much retail space at Low Pavement would prejudice later redevelopment elsewhere in the town centre. Better to spread development resources over a wider area, they argued. In effect, they were putting a strong economic case for an incremental development strategy. And, of course, such an approach sits better with conservation objectives.

Fig 35 Feilden & Mawson scheme. Courtyard
south of No 41 Low Pavement

Fig 36 Feilden & Mawson scheme. View of
shopping mall from Low Pavement

Four other points were strongly in the minds of the Working Party and its consultants. The first had to do with continuity of shop fronts. Gaps in shopping frontage, whether in new malls or refurbished and converted buildings, discourage shoppers from walking any further; they are to be avoided.

Secondly, the study team was keenly aware of a conflict between the conservation objective of keeping buildings rather than just facades and the requirements of prospective tenants for wide, clear-span spaces without columns or dividing walls. It had to be recognised that, in the ordinary way, retaining the internal character of the existing Low Pavement buildings would cut the rent levels that could be asked for them.

Funders' requirements

Thirdly, whereas in many areas of conservation, refurbishment which guarantees a 20-year or even 10-year life may be acceptable, for the funding of large-scale retail development it is not. The funders demand a building which has a life expectation comparable to new-build. And, finally, the same principle applies to management and maintenance. Odd-shaped interiors and difficult-to-maintain surfaces may be assets in a restaurant, wine bar, or private home; but they have little charm for a retail developer or for tenants if they result in spiralling service charges.

The Working Party and its sub-groups proceeded remarkably briskly. The full Working Party met three times between January and mid-March 1976; on 25 March it made a slide presentation to the Steering Group; in April it hammered out its report; in May it submitted the final version to the Steering Group.

It followed this in June with an informal presentation to council members, at which the Town Clerk Ralph Kennedy skilfully deployed the arguments against. Ostensibly he spoke as 'devil's advocate'; in reality he remained convinced that a clear-and-rebuild scheme would best ensure Chesterfield's prosperity. By this time, however, the tide was flowing too strongly against him.

In the same month the borough council's Policy Committee, the county council's Area Planning Committee, and the Borough Planning and Estates Committee all considered the proposals for conservation area designation. This was important, not only symbolically and for the additional control it gave the council, but for the promise it held out of historic buildings grants to help restore key frontage buildings in Low Pavement.

The public consulted

Brisk though the pace was, the study team took pains to consult the public. They met representatives of amenity and traders' organisations and sent out 350 questionnaires to schools and clubs in the town. The questionnaires were aimed at discovering how people – including especially young people – perceived their town and what they wanted of it. The consultants concluded that Chesterfield folk had an affection for, but an inferiority complex about, their town. This was no doubt due in large measure to the poor quality of redevelopment that had occurred and the slough of despond into which the main redevelopment proposals had sunk.

41

Fig 37　Low Pavement frontage, 1973, prior to restoration

Fig 38　Market Hall prior to restoration

Fig 39　Market Hall prior to restoration

At the beginning of July the full council endorsed the Policy Committee's recommendation that it launch consultation with an exhibition of development alternatives. These were the two Bernard Engel schemes, the Enterprise Developments scheme, and the Feilden & Mawson conservation alternative. Significantly, the council decided that the exhibition must make clear its own preference for the F & M scheme.

The council launched its public participation exercise in late July 1976 with an exhibition based on the Working Party report. This took place from 26 to 31 July at the then public library just off Market Place, and included plans and perspectives illustrating the Working Party's ideas for redeveloping Low Pavement as well as the Engel and Enterprise Developments schemes.

A choice of designs

The exhibition went hand in hand with circulation of the report to local organisations, including the Chamber of Trade, Market Traders Federation, Civic Society, Heritage Society, and Chamber of Commerce. The exercise culminated in a public meeting at the Assembly Room in the Market Hall on 30 July attended by 120 people, at which the designers of the four schemes explained them and answered questions on them.

More than 1500 people visited the six-day exhibition, of whom 344 filled in comment sheets. Of these 271 (80%) favoured the scheme designed by Feilden & Mawson and recommended by the Working Party. Next most popular was the locally generated Enterprise Developments scheme, chosen by 33 respondents (9%). The two Bernard Engel schemes scored only 5% and 1%, with 5% expressing no preference. The Working Party's approach had gained a clear endorsement from public opinion.

A vote for conservation

The replies made it clear that the overwhelming reason why people liked the Feilden & Mawson scheme was its retention of the town's character, its old buildings, and Market Hall, and its convincing indication that this could be combined with improved facilities. The Civic and Heritage Societies and the Market Traders all supported the Working Party's recommendations; the two amenity societies urged the council to retain Feilden & Mawson as consultant architects for the town centre redevelopment.

The main opposition came from the Chamber of Trade which preferred the Enterprise Developments scheme. This, it believed, could be completed more quickly and with less disturbance to traders; it also approved of that scheme's large car park and local financial involvement. The Chamber believed that retention of the Market Hall and the Low Pavement frontage buildings would make for less efficiency (Figs 37–40).

Newspaper comment and letters to editors generally favoured the report, though the *Derbyshire Times* did not support retention of the Market Hall. Almost everyone approved of the report's proposals for upgrading and refurbishment of the Market Place and The Shambles.

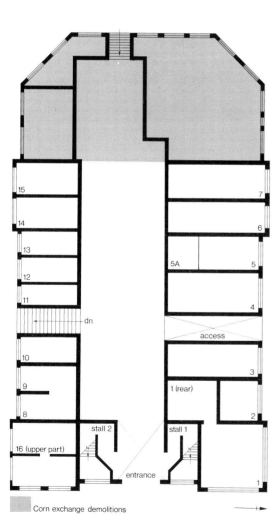

Fig 40   Plan of Market Hall prior to reorganisation and extension

6 So will it work?

On 29 September 1976 the council's Policy General Sub-Committee met, noted the views expressed by public and local organisations, and passed a four paragraph resolution. This:

- accepted the feasibility of retaining the front section of the Low Pavement buildings;
- recommended the council to accept the Working Party report;
- recommended the council to enlarge the conservation area, and apply to the DoE to recognise it as 'outstanding'; and
- asked Feilden & Mawson, quantity surveyors Summers & Partners, and appropriate council officers to advise whether refurbishment of the Market Hall could economically provide the necessary improved facilities.

This recommendation was then debated at a meeting of the full council on 5 October 1976. It unanimously endorsed the recommendations and invited Feilden & Mawson to continue as conservation consultants.

The great black elephant

Much effort during the remainder of 1976 went into devising a workable answer to the problem of the Market Hall. Despite all the efforts of Feilden & Mawson, there was widespread reluctance among both public and council to believe that this great black elephant could have any future. They may be forgiven for writing the building off. No less an authority than Pevsner called it 'the crudest show of high Victorian provincial prosperity' (Fig 41). However, surveys showed it to be not only structurally sound but, under its grime, rather a handsome and impressive building.

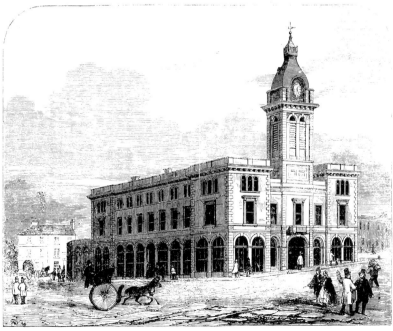

NEW MARKET-HALL, CHESTERFIELD.

Fig 41   Market Hall on completion in 1857

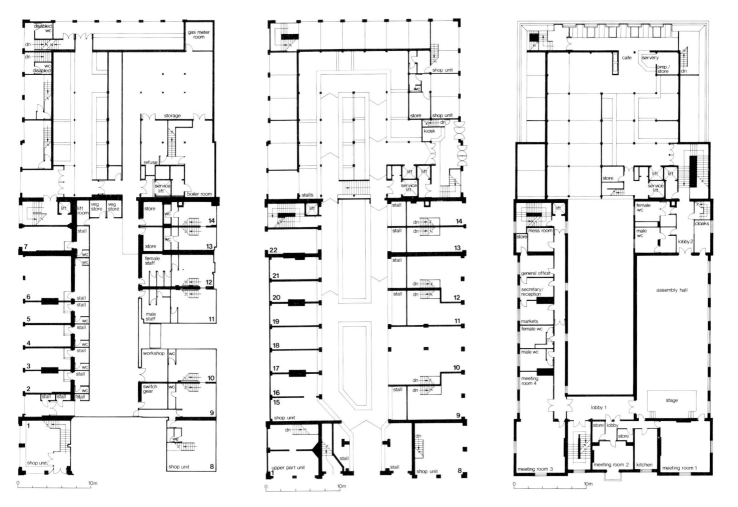

Fig 42   Market Hall scheme prepared in 1977 by J Belchamber, former Chief Architect, Technical Services Department, Chesterfield Borough Council. Lower ground level, ground level, and first floor level

Covered accommodation for some 70 market stalls was needed; three options offered themselves:

– demolish and replace with a new building
– refurbish the whole building
– part refurbish, part demolish, and rebuild

Cheaper to keep it

The consultants' original preference was for keeping and refurbishing the whole building. They were convinced that this was both desirable on architectural/townscape grounds and a more economical solution than demolition and rebuilding.

Their initial proposals used the building's underused upper storeys to provide a second level of stalls. This, however, required building regulation approval. Applied flexibly these regulations could probably have made this possible; but there was a strong body of opinion in the Town Hall which saw no virtue in the building's retention. This persisted despite decisions in principle to refurbish. At one point it fell to the DoE's Philip Waddington to point out to a Steering Group meeting which was clearly wavering that any new market hall ought to be on the same site, and a new market hall there had been shown to be more expensive than retention of the existing building.

Fig 43 Market Hall scheme, 1977, showing the proposed extension

Ambiguous building regulations

The building regulations at that time displayed some ambiguity as to whether, when a building was altered, they applied with full force only to the reconstructed parts or to the entire building. The critical issue was combustibility of existing timber floors to the upper storeys. To ensure one-hour-plus fire resistance, the then regulations stipulated that materials should be wholly non-combustible except in buildings less than 15m high. The consultants made a case that, with fire resisting vertical divisions to exclude the clock tower, they could bring the actual Market Hall within the 15m limit. The council's building inspector reached the opposite conclusion, and was not willing to recommend a waiver.

Fig 44 Market Hall reconstruction in progress, 1979

46

The part refurbish/part rebuild solution which F & M adopted neatly sidestepped this issue. Demolition of the architecturally inferior west end of the building made way for a new two-storey market building in which the regulations applied most stringently, but with maximum scope for new facilities. In the old building, only the original Market Hall was used, albeit with its space reorganised and ramps introduced to link up and down with the new building. Upper storeys were retained as meeting rooms but upgraded.

Thus, because there was no effective change of use in either upper or lower storeys, the regulations applied less stringently and refurbishment costs could be kept within acceptable limits. Yet the old and new buildings work effectively as one Market Hall (Figs 42, 43). The detailed design and contract supervision were undertaken by the council's own architects, and the refurbishment element attracted some DoE historic buildings grant aid. The total cost was £1.5m. It was estimated that clear-and-rebuild would have cost about 20% more. Work started in November 1978 (Fig 44) and the transformed market reopened for trading in autumn 1980.

Money for redevelopment

As to the main shopping redevelopment, the council, having opted for a conservation approach, now had to make it work financially. In other circumstances it might itself have found the money to build the scheme; as it was, spending restrictions and other capital commitments ruled this out. To raise the required capital, it had two options.

Option A was for it to take a partner development company, give it a long ground lease, and hand over responsibility for the development to that company in return for an annual ground rent, reviewable in the light of income. This way the council would hand over the risks but would also hand over control of detailed design and lettings.

Option B was to agree a direct funding arrangement with an institution such as a pension fund, giving it a long lease at a peppercorn rent, but then taking a lease-back from the institution at a rent set to give it its required return. This way the council would accept some of

Fig 45 Scheme for Boots store, showing the integration of the Low Pavement frontage with the new shopping development (prepared in 1980 by J H Gant, former Chief Architect, Boots, in association with Elsom Pack Roberts, architects for the main development. Ground level, first floor level, and second floor level

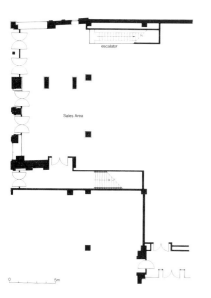

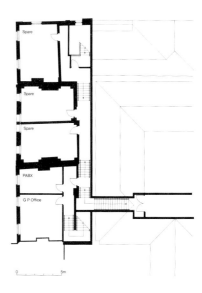

the risk, but would be likely to receive a higher yield – though probably not in the years before the first rent review. It would also assume the final responsibility for letting the scheme, and would have a greater responsibility for getting the design right.

Sizing up developers

In the circumstances of a property market just beginning to revive after its 1973 collapse, economic consultants Goddard & Smith recommended the council to keep both options open, and officers began to approach a selection of developers and institutions. It may be significant that rather fewer than half of the 30-odd companies approached expressed interest; but from the 16 interviewed came a short-list of six. These council officers vetted for financial soundness,

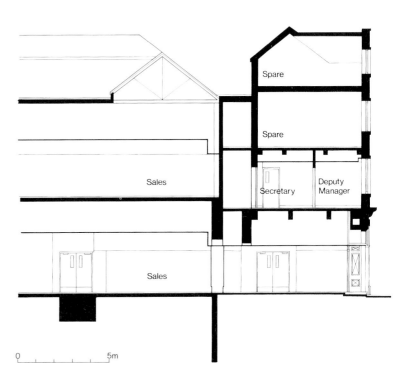

Fig 46   Scheme for Boots store. Section

Fig 47   Scheme for Boots store. Section

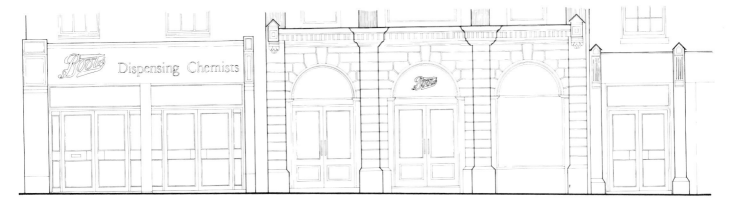

Fig 48   Scheme for Boots store. Elevation. Note the retention of the individual frontages

previous experience, attitudes to conservation, and likely financial terms. At the end of this process it became clear that CIN Properties Ltd – the property arm of the Coal Board pension fund – must be the choice. In terms of readiness to accept a conservation approach and offer an acceptable financial deal, none of the others was in the running.

A deal agreed

The deal now struck was as follows:

– Chesterfield council secures 'pre-let' tenants for the two anchor stores – the supermarket and the variety store.
– It then leases the entire Low Pavement site to CIN for 125 years at a peppercorn rent.
– CIN builds a shopping centre in accordance with agreed plans, specifications, and timetable.
– When it is completed, CIN leases it back to the council for the remainder of the 125 years less three days.
– Out of its rent-roll, the council pays CIN a rent equal to its required return.
– After the first rent review, the council and CIN share the rent income in the same proportions as in the first year.

Letting the supermarket

To cross the first hurdle, the council invited tenders from prospective tenants of the supermarket, to be sited at the western end of the development and occupying 3700 sq m (40,000 sq ft) out of a total of 16,000 sq m (174,000 sq ft). It was in a strong position because of the lack of any other suitable sites in the town, and was able to choose between three bidders. The sealed tender from Macfisheries (later International and now Gateway), equivalent to £65 per sq m, came out top.

For the other anchor store at the eastern end, both the amount of space and the way in which it fitted in behind the retail Low Pavement properties were more open to negotiation. This slot evoked less interest from potential tenants. Eventually the council agreed terms with Boots, who needed between 3700 and 4700 sq m (40–50,000 sq ft).

Fig 49 (*above*) and **Fig 50** (*below*) Boots store showing contrasting treatment of the shopfronts

Boots agree to keep old buildings

They were agreeable to most of this being in the new building but wanted a presence (entrance plus shop windows) on Low Pavement. To achieve this, they agreed to take space in listed buildings, even though in this front 6m of their premises they would not have the floor-to-ceiling heights they normally insist on.

As for the upper storeys of these listed buildings, council officers and consultants then persuaded the company to use these for staff accommodation, offices, and other ancillary uses. These negotiations were not easy, but were of immense value in demonstrating that such accommodation can, by breaking it down into quite small units, be satisfactorily housed in small-scale existing buildings (Figs 45–50).

Executive architects chosen

Though CIN accepted the Feilden & Mawson scheme, they thought it necessary to commission a practice experienced in large shopping schemes as executive architects. They chose the Elsom Pack Roberts Partnership, who were to work in close association with Feilden & Mawson, the council's conservation consultants. This relationship expressed an inevitable tension between conservation objectives and utilitarian objectives based on what the executive architects saw as practical and economic. It required give-and-take on both sides, with the joint clients – council and CIN – sometimes being called on to adjudicate.

Perhaps the most significant departures from Feilden & Mawson's outline proposals made by the executive architects stemmed from Elsom Pack Roberts' conviction that a megastructure – in this case, a single concrete-framed shopping building – was necessary in order to provide an efficient main shopping mall and servicing. The conservation penalty from this course was to make it more difficult to stitch in the retained Low Pavement buildings.

Excavation for the servicing areas, for instance, required demolition of more of the rear portions of these buildings than the conservation consultants had originally envisaged (Fig 51). But though some

Fig 51 Shopping development known as 'The Pavements' under construction in 1979 and incorporating the existing Low Pavement frontage (architect Elsom Pack Roberts)

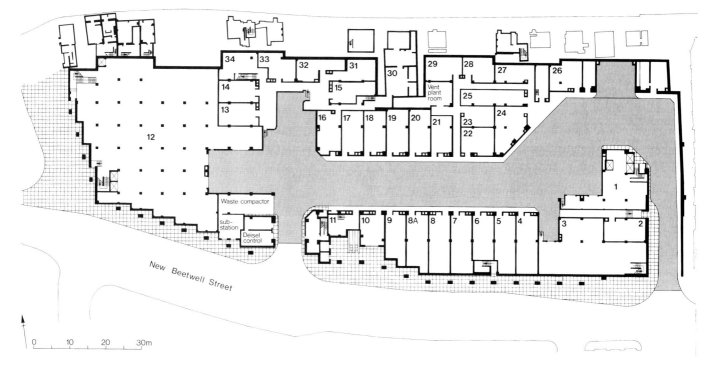

Fig 52 Scheme for 'The Pavements' shopping development prepared in 1978 by architects Elsom Pack Roberts. Service basement, New Beetwell Street level

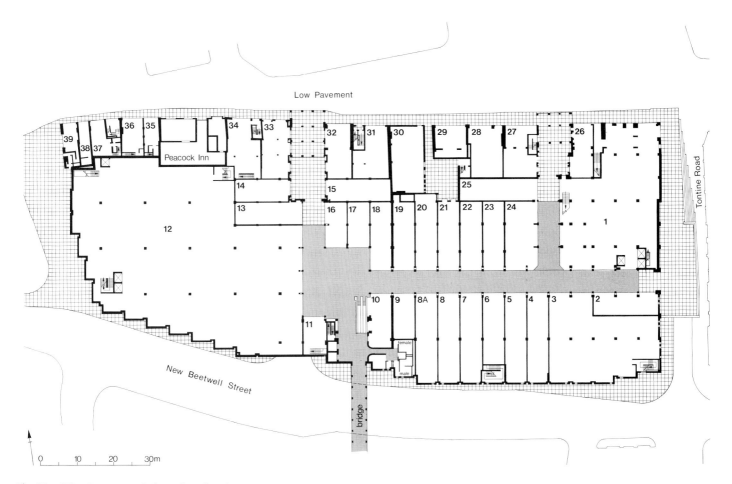

Fig 53 'The Pavements' shopping development. Mall/Low Pavement level

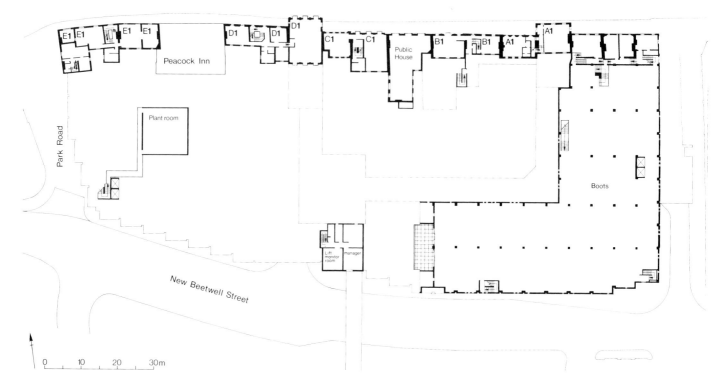

Fig 54 'The Pavements' shopping development. **First floor**

Fig 55 'The Pavements' shopping development. **Section**

interesting older structures had to go, in townscape terms there was little loss. The retained Low Pavement frontages had enough depth of building behind them to carry conviction. And in terms of facing materials – brick and slate – and elevations and roofscape, Feilden & Mawson's ideas were generally implemented.

A more commercial view

Other changes concerned the nature of the shopping mall, which Geoffrey Mitchell had envisaged as curving round somewhat behind Low Pavement and consisting of a series of covered sections with intervening points – courtyards, alleys, and so on – at which the shopper saw daylight and felt fresh air.

In the event, the expert commercial view of likely trading patterns, efficient maintenance routines, and shopper reaction prevailed. It dictated that the mall be straight, completely covered in, and with only three public access routes towards Low Pavement. For the lofty, glazed barrel vaults suggested by Mitchell, the executive architects substituted solid and relatively low ceilings. The Pavements is very much an enclosed space with little or no visual connection with the outside world (Figs 52–64).

Fig 56   The Low Pavement frontage restored

Fig 57   The Low Pavement frontage restored

Fig 58   The Low Pavement frontage seen from Market Place after restoration

Fig 59 'The Pavements' shopping development. Link between the Market Place and the new shopping mall

Fig 60 'The Pavements' shopping development. The new shopping mall

Fig 61 'The Pavements' shopping development. Escalator link to New Beetwell Street and buses

Fig 62 'The Pavements' shopping development. Sitting area with direct links to Low Pavement, the new shopping mall, the car park, and buses

Fig 63 'The Pavements' shopping development. Elevation to New Beetwell Street

Fig 64 Upper floor space over shops in Low Pavement back in intensive use for offices

The Pavements goes ahead

By August 1978 matters were far enough advanced for council leader Bill Flanagan to announce that The Pavements (as the development was now to be called) was going ahead. The Secretary of State for the Environment had given the scheme planning permission; the Royal Fine Art Commission had given it its fulsome blessing. It considered it 'a model of the way in which this sort of problem could be solved' and offered Chesterfield its congratulations. The result, the RFAC believed, would 'justify the trials and efforts of the last five years.'

A model of what?

When the Commission described Chesterfield's new approach as 'a model', we may assume it was thinking not just of the refurbishment and infill approach to the main shopping building, but of what had now emerged as a concerted programme of redevelopment, refurbishment, and enhancement. This included plans to repave and upgrade the Market Place, enhancement in the conservation area generally, repaving and improvement in The Shambles area as a stimulus to work by property owners in what had been a blighted area, plans by the county to build a new library east of The Pavements, and further phases of shopping redevelopment. In some ways most significant here was what were then called the 'Stage 2' proposals for the area behind Central Pavement to be tackled essentially on a building-by-building basis rather than by imposition of a single 'megastructure'.

But Central Pavement was for the future. In 1979 the prime objective was to achieve the essential injection of new shopping at minimum conservation cost. The agreed demolition of the back buildings behind Low Pavement started in September; the main contract started in January 1979, with Sir Robert McAlpine as main contractor. The value of CIN's work (leaving aside capital works by the council) came to some £12.5m.

Fig 65   The Market Hall restored, 1981

Work had, as we have seen, already started on the refurbishment and part replacement of the Market Hall. As the builders, Fairclough, scraped the grime from its brickwork and began to repair its external decorative features, councillors and townspeople began belatedly to rediscover the handsome building that the conservation consultants had all along known was there.

Market Hall reopens

In November 1980 the Market Hall – with its replacement western section, ramped and reorganised interior, refurbished assembly room complete with Victorian wall tiles, and meeting rooms and offices – was officially opened. Behind all the detailed argument about fire resistance and refurbishment costs had lain Feilden & Mawson's conviction that here was a building which in visual terms it would be difficult or impossible to replace at acceptable cost. With its clock tower and dominant facade to the Market Place, it formed one of the lynch-pins of the Chesterfield townscape (Figs 65–67).

Fig 66   The Market Hall restored, 1981

Fig 67   The Market Hall. New western extension

Fig 68   Opening of the Market Hall and 'The Pavements' shopping development by the Prince and Princess of Wales, 1981

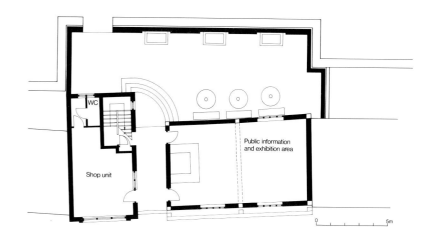

Fig 69 The Peacock. Scheme prepared in 1977 for restoration, extension, and conversion to tourist office and heritage centre (architect, J Belchamber, former Chief Architect, Technical Services Department, Chesterfield Borough Council. Architectural Consultant for restoration, F W B Charles). Ground level

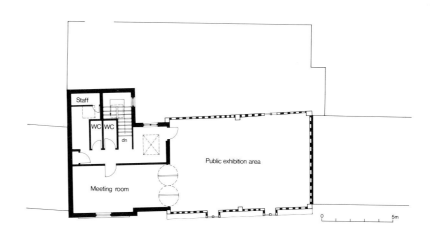

Fig 70 The Peacock scheme. First floor

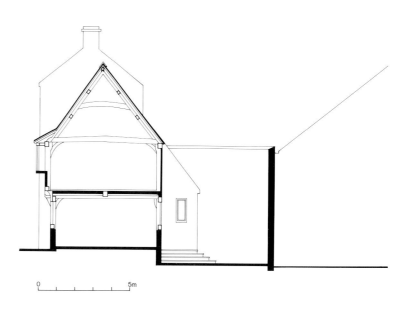

Fig 71 The Peacock scheme. Section

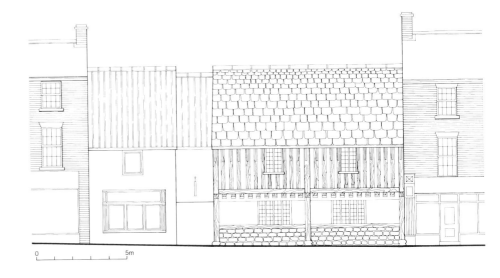

Fig 72   The Peacock scheme. Elevation to Low Pavement

Fig 73   The Peacock. Low Pavement frontage

Fig 74   The Peacock. Rear courtyard

Fig 75   The Peacock. Water feature

Fig 76   The Peacock. First floor heritage centre

A 'heart transplant'

This view was now triumphantly vindicated. An enthusiastic press described the operation as 'a heart transplant'. This description applied with even more force to The Pavements, completed in June 1981 and officially opened that November by the Prince and Princess of Wales (Fig 68).

The town centre which the royal visitors saw on that occasion was also the better for three other improvements carried out more or less simultaneously. First, the Peacock, whose listing had proved a key factor in delaying and ultimately preventing wholesale demolitions on Low Pavement, was restored to its full glory and given a useful new role. It and a new building, on an adjoining vacant site which had been part of the Peacock, were turned into a tourist information and heritage centre which is well located for its function and helps and is helped by visitor-oriented shops and restaurants on the Low Pavement frontage. It now stands out as a cardinal element in the Low Pavement frontage, a building self-evidently meriting preservation (Figs 69–76).

Fig 77   Market Place. Repaired granite setts

Fig 78   Low Pavement. Sunken paving in York stone

Fig 79   Market stall with coloured canvas roof

Fig 80   Market stalls seen from the Market Hall

Repaving the squares

Secondly the council carried out a comprehensive scheme of repaving for the Market Place (Fig 77) and New Square, whose stone setts had suffered from lack of maintenance, defective drainage, and unsympathetic patching with tarmac. Feilden & Mawson had stressed the importance to people's perceptions of the centre of appropriate, good quality surfaces underfoot.

Low Pavement is so called because the actual stone-paved footway is at one point below the level of the adjoining road. No pretext of tidiness or public liability was allowed to discourage the council from retaining this distinctive feature. The programme of relaying and repair of the traditional setts, though it encountered some practical difficulties, both provided that sense of quality and reinforced the sense of traditional character conserved (Fig 78).

Other ingredients of the overall market square improvement (Figs 79, 80) included the installation of a nineteenth-century fountain as a visual focus and source of movement in the otherwise sometimes bleak New Square (Fig 81), the restoration of the rather grand and idiosyncratic nineteenth-century town pump (carried out free of charge by Markhams, a local engineering company) (Fig 82), retention and refurbishment of original nineteenth-century lamp-posts (Fig 83), and more seats.

Fig 81   New Square. Resited fountain

Fig 82   Market Place. Town pump

Fig 83   Low Pavement. Listed lamp standard

Fig 84   Multi-storey car park linking with 'The Pavements' shopping development (architects, Feilden & Mawson)

Cutting down the traffic

Thirdly, new traffic regulations cut the number of vehicles penetrating into the two squares by restricting entry in peak periods to market traders and those with a need for access (including vehicles carrying disabled people). This went hand in hand with the opening that April 1982 of the New Beetwell Street multi-storey car park.

This building, designed by Feilden & Mawson, provided 500 car spaces and was directly linked by bridge to The Pavements. It cost £1.6m, and Geoffrey Mitchell's concept of a brick mill or warehouse with window openings separated vertically and broken by decorative steel grills showed that such structures need not be ugly concrete layer cakes (Figs 84–86).

Honours thick and fast

Honours now came thick and fast: a Europa Nostra Medal in 1981, one of only five awarded that year in all Europe; an RICS/*The Times* Conservation Award for the Market Hall in 1981, followed by a commendation for The Pavements in 1982; and the only Derbyshire Civic Trust Award in 1982 for the overall redevelopment of the town centre (Fig 87). Others came from the Conservation Foundation, the Business in Industry Panel for the Environment, the Concrete Society, the Mark Henig Awards for tourism enterprise, the 1982 Otis Awards, and – in some ways especially welcome – the CARE award, sponsored in association with the Civic Trust Awards by developers Grosvenor Estates and MEPC, for 'an outstanding example of urban renewal in the United Kingdom'.

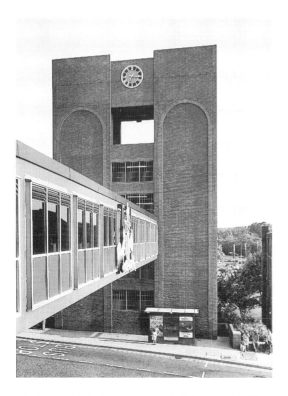

Fig 85   Multi-storey car park linking with 'The Pavements' shopping development (architects, Feilden & Mawson)

Fig 86   Multi-storey car park linking with 'The Pavements' shopping development (architects, Feilden & Mawson)

Fig 87   Awards for 'The Pavements' shopping development, the Market Hall restoration, and for conservation work in the town centre

7 Building on success

The importance of The Pavements lies not just in the addition of much needed new shopping to the town centre; it also concerns what development economists call 'critical mass'. Below a certain size, the snowball melts as it rolls; above that crucial size it hardens the snow it gathers.

The council and its conservation consultants had accepted compromises to their original conservation objectives, in the shape of a closed-in megastructure, less of the traditional north–south 'grain' of alleys and passageways, and more extensive replacement of fabric in the repair of the Low Pavement buildings than they would have wished.

This, however, was – in the climate of the 1970s – the price for securing the confidence and involvement of a funding institution willing to go along with a broadly conservation approach, and thus the price of being able to achieve the 'critical mass' which would turn round Chesterfield's retail fortunes, bring in more shoppers, and provide the confidence and development potential to achieve the wider economic and environmental objectives pinpointed by the consultants.

Other developments follow

During the years since the opening of The Pavements a number of other, smaller-scale developments and improvements, described below, have been achieved or set in motion which have had a cumulative but profound impact on the image, morale, and prosperity of the town centre. This prosperity has prompted prospects for a second major town centre redevelopment on the Vicar Lane site, east of The Shambles. This too is described below.

Extending the 'paved zone'

The council has gradually extended the pedestrian priority shopping zone and repaved lengths of street running out of the two main squares. Feilden & Mawson stressed early on the effect of good quality repaving on the image of a town centre. In subconsciously forming an impression of environmental quality, most shoppers are primarily influenced by what they see at eye level and feel under their feet. The quality of shop-fronts, fascias, and street furniture and the colour, texture, and state of repair of the surface they walk on are all crucial. Money spent on upgrading and maintaining paving should be regarded by councillors, ratepayers, and indeed central government as a thoroughly sound investment for any competitive shopping centre (Fig 88).

Fig 88 Market Place free of traffic and parked cars. 'No Parking Zone' perimeter signs obviate the need for yellow lines

Traffic growth and changes in pedestrian zone

One of the reasons for proposing a major town centre redevelopment scheme in the 1950s was the wish to resolve problems of traffic congestion. Ironically, by the time the council eventually began building The Pavements, much had been done to remove major traffic flows from the centre.

Nonetheless, buses as well as servicing vehicles and general traffic still penetrated the market square, cutting New Square in half; buses still used High Street/Burlington Street. After some debate the study team proposed removal of buses from the market square and closure of the diagonal road across New Square. High Street/Burlington Street had already been closed to servicing traffic between 10am and 5pm; this continued.

The arrangements adopted catered for servicing and access traffic by creating two one-way loops, one south of Knifesmithgate, and one north of Beetwell Street. Traffic could thus reach both the south (Low Pavement) side of the market area and the north (High Street/New Square) side; but tough limits on parking removed the motive for most drivers to use these loops (Fig 89).

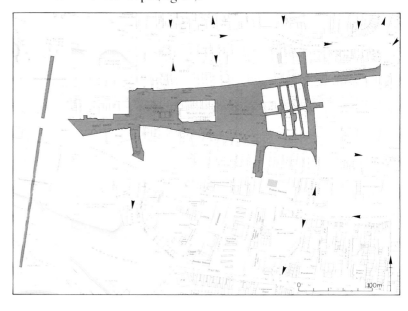

Fig 89 Pedestrian priority area and one-way streets

It should be noted that the council avoided the rash of double yellow lines which normally attend such a regime by use of sections 54 and 55 of the 1967 Road Traffic Regulation Act. This allows a local authority, where the Secretary of State accepts that there are special environmental reasons, to dispense with yellow lines and simply mark a control zone with 'No Parking' notices.

Since the council introduced the original traffic and parking regime in 1981, access and servicing traffic has grown steadily; so have visits by disabled persons' vehicles. These increases threatened to damage the 'minimum traffic' environment created by the original orders. In 1988, therefore, the borough council embarked upon a two-pronged approach: to improve car parking facilities for disabled people on the edge of the pedestrian zone, and at the same time to ban all traffic from Low Pavement (including the disabled and servicing vehicles) from 10am to 4pm.

The result, says Michael Kennedy, will be to create a virtually traffic-free pedestrian precinct including the two market squares, Low and Central Pavements, Packer's Row, and High Street. Traffic penetration at these times will be limited to the Glumangate–Soresby Street loop and a cul-de-sac on the north side of New Square.

Reviving a Shambles

The council's commitment to conserving the Shambles area with its medieval pattern of narrow lanes and alleys found tangible expression in a scheme to repave virtually throughout in stone setts after extensive

Fig 90 The Shambles. Plan showing new and restored buildings and repaving

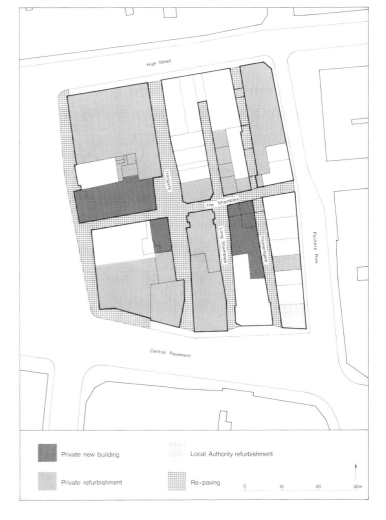

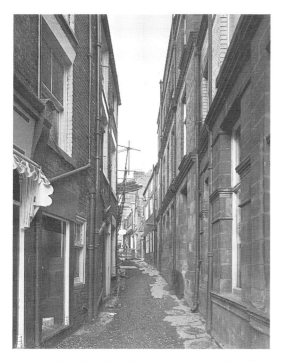

Fig 91 The Shambles in 1979 prior to rehabilitation

Fig 92   The Shambles in 1979 prior to rehabilitation

repair and relaying of drains. This commitment, together with a firm, clear policy of conserve and repair as opposed to clear-and-rebuild, encouraged a key property owner, S E Redfern Ltd, to upgrade its buildings and rebuild on a gap site (Figs 90–94).

Redfern's properties consisted of a terrace of derelict shops and partly demolished buildings at the heart of the grid of narrow streets which forms The Shambles. The company's original instinct was to demolish more than they ultimately did; the council, on the advice of its conservation consultants and planning and estates officer, pushed for maximum retention of existing buildings, even where they were in a state of disrepair or dereliction, in order to retain the feel of The Shambles, which would have been weakened by more new-build, however sympathetic.

Redferns engaged Sheffield architects Hadfield Cawkwell Davidson & Partners (who knew the town centre from design studies they had done for abortive shopping redevelopment schemes) to design and supervise the regeneration of their properties. Once schemes involving more than minimum demolition had been discarded, project architect Mike Brearley and partner Alan Baggaley were able to concentrate on a conservationist scheme which retained the external structure of the buildings. These were stripped back to their structural shell, then reroofed, refloored, and plastered to give tenants a basic shell for fitting out. Town scheme grants, with borough and county contributing to match the HBC/DoE money, helped to meet the cost of cast-iron rainwater pipes and gutters, slates, and hand-made bricks.

The Grade II listing of the terrace specifically mentions a timber bressumer spanning a minor alleyway, which therefore had to be retained. The architects also managed to keep bowed brickwork over this beam, though it required some skilful structural engineering detailing to do so while relieving the load on the venerable beam. Hadfield Cawkwell Davidson provided their own structural engineer.

Fig 93   The Shambles in 1979 prior to rehabilitation

Fig 94   The Shambles restored

Fig 95 The Shambles restored

In designing the infill building, the architects first studied roof pitches of adjoining buildings and their relationship to the street. However, instead of following the style of these brick vernacular buildings, they aimed at catching the spirit of the medieval, half-timbered Royal Oak pub opposite (Fig 95). The new building has overhanging eaves, brick corbelling for a projecting second storey, and timber oriel windows nestling under its eaves (Fig 96). As the buildings entirely fill their site, soft landscaping was not possible; instead the architects continued the existing stone flags round its other sides.

The feasibility of the scheme as built was established in 1979 after several years of discussion and redesign; work started in 1980 and was completed and substantially let in 1981. Alan Baggaley says that he and his colleagues would not, even with the benefit of hindsight, have changed very much. Their only regrets are that tenants have not produced as good a standard of shopfronts and signs as could have been achieved with tighter control, which they believe 'would have paid dividends' and that statutory undertakers have since made a mess in digging up the paving to gain access to services.

Fig 96 The Shambles restored

Public library

The next substantial building to be slotted into the town centre was the new public library. Derbyshire's libraries service under county librarian Peter Gratton had for some years pursued a policy of siting libraries whenever possible in shopping centres, and the site made available in Chesterfield – immediately to the east of The Pavements – met this criterion admirably.

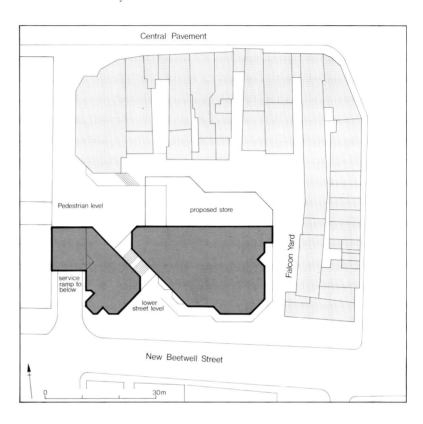

Fig 97 Scheme for Chesterfield Public Library, 1981 (R G Geall, former County Architect, Derbyshire County Council: job architect, M H Chapman). Site plan

The library, designed by the county architect's department (Figs 97–102), built at a cost of £3m, and opened in 1985, like The Pavements occupies a steeply sloping site. Its main entrance is within a few yards of the eastern entrance of the main shopping mall and, in addition to traditional library facilities such as lending and reference departments, it has a coffee bar, video loan section, and computer terminals for public information use. The public pedestrian route linking The Pavements and the market square to New Beetwell Street bus stops runs as a wide flight of steps diagonally through the building starting close to its main (Tontine Road) entrance (Fig 103); coffee bar and meeting rooms are at the lower Beetwell Street level and can be open via the separate entrance there when the rest of the building is closed.

While there has been some debate as to how well the building fits in to the Chesterfield townscape, there can be little doubt that it is very much better used than the previous library buildings – the main Stephenson Memorial Library in Corporation Street and the children's library tucked away off New Square. In the first full year of operation, its adult membership was, at 49,800, 58% up on membership in the last full year of the old library; children's membership at 17,800 was 53% up. Book loans to adults were 53% up, to children 84% up; video loans were 370% up. The adult book stock was half as big again, the

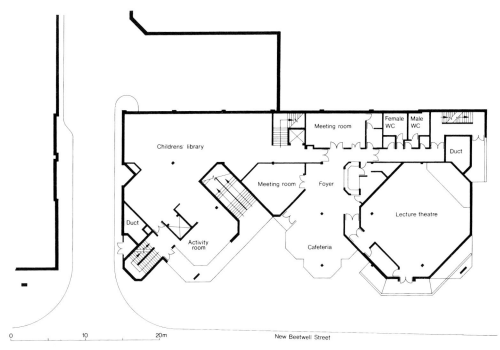

Fig 98 Chesterfield Public Library. New Beet-well Street level

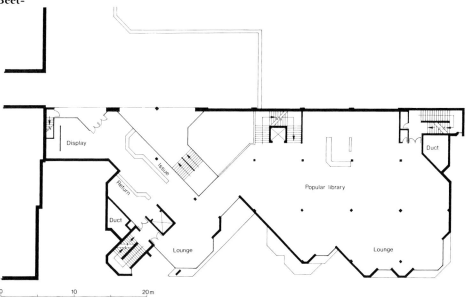

Fig 99 Chesterfield Public Library. 'The Pavements' mall level

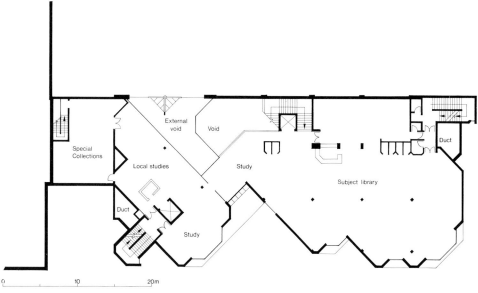

Fig 100 Chesterfield Public Library. Upper level

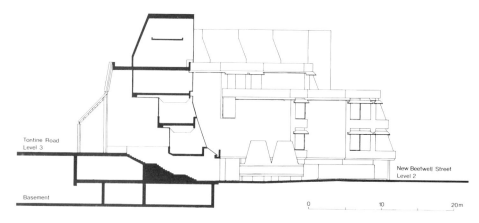

Fig 101 Chesterfield Public Library. Section/elevation

children's book stock 35% up, video-tapes 82% up; and it now also stocked 380 items of computer software. The building has also proved a popular venue for meetings; in its first full year 87 different organisations held meetings there on 968 occasions. In 1988 it beat more than 500 other libraries to gain an award sponsored by Radio 4 and a library supplier and judged by the votes of library users for quality of service; it has also won an RIBA regional award.

Much of this no doubt reflects superior facilities and a much greater floorspace (3900 sq m, 42,000 sq ft, against the previous 1400 sq m, 15,000 sq ft). But the dramatic increase in use also reflects its key position at the junction of two pedestrian routes, close both to The Pavements and bus stops, and very visible from the Market Place. It also seems clear – though it is difficult to prove – that the library helps the shopping centre as well as shopping boosting the library's 'turnover'.

Fig 102 Chesterfield Public Library. Interior

Fig 103 Chesterfield Public Library. Public stairway linking 'The Pavements' mall level to New Beetwell Street

Central Pavement

Central Pavement is, strictly speaking, the eastward continuation of Low Pavement – that is, a row of frontage buildings and the stone-paved footway (pavement) at their doors. The name, however, became attached to an area of lanes, alleys, and buildings running back and down from those frontage buildings. This area, less the site earmarked for the library, was an obvious target for a further stage in town centre regeneration – especially if a pedestrian route could be created to extend the flow through the main shopping mall of The Pavements.

The council and its consultants, moreover, saw this Central Pavement area as the opportunity to practice the kind of small-scale, restore and infill conservation that had proved economically impossible in the initial development. The area has in practice been tackled in three stages: its central core, running back from the Central Pavement frontage into the historic but decayed Theatre Yard; an infill development to link Theatre Yard to Tontine Road and The Pavements; and the redevelopment, by a mixture of refurbishment and new-build, of the area east of Theatre Yard between it and South Street, known as Falcon Yard (Figs 104–107).

The first stage ('Theatre Yard') tackled four three-storey buildings owned by the council, which formed part of the terrace fronting on to

Fig 104 Proposals for Central Pavement and South Street, 1982, prepared by Chesterfield Borough Council and their consultants Feilden & Mawson

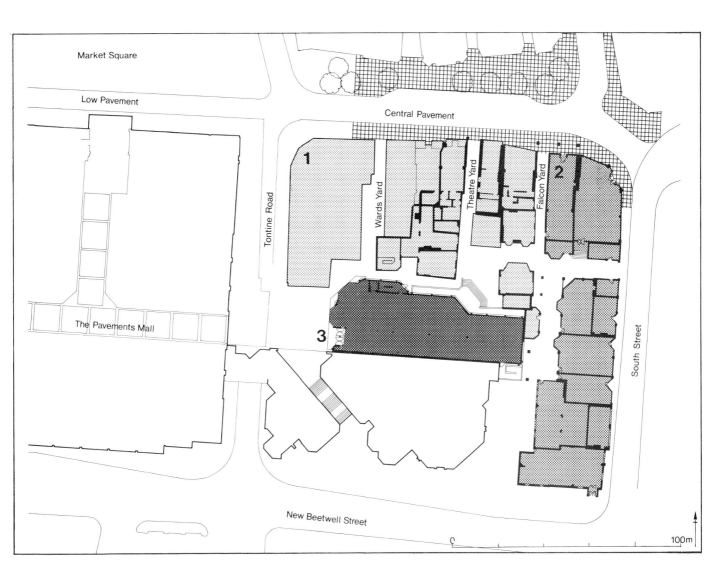

Fig 105   Central Pavement frontage in 1982 prior to restoration showing listed shops

Fig 106   Listed shop-front in Central Pavement, 1982

Fig 107   Listed shop interior with Art Nouveau tiling

Central Pavement and were visible from the Market Place, together with their two-storey back extensions. These rear extensions opened on to Theatre Yard and Falcon Yard, two of the typical lanes which connected through archways with Central Pavement. Three of the four buildings were listed Grade II, the fourth was on the advisory local list.

The front buildings, visible from the Market Place, on a well-used pedestrian route, and in a relatively good state of repair, could be tackled fairly straightforwardly. The refurbishment approach here was relatively conservative, with functional improvements limited to those required by prospective tenants rather than linked to some notional standard necessary to attract funding or satisfy multiples.

The four front shop units were all fairly quickly let, and one which became vacant was relet – unexpectedly – to a bookseller, Alan Hill, who had for some time sought suitable premises in Chesterfield. By 1988 he had done sufficiently well to contemplate opening separate secondhand and remainder bookshops nearby. The opening and survival of an independent, specialist bookshop may be regarded as a litmus test of a town centre's transition from a defensive, limited retail

Fig 108   Central Pavement after restoration

Fig 109   Central Pavement. New planting, paving, and lamp-posts

range to a booming and varied retail range. It shows that quality and specialist traders are beginning to draw in shoppers from a much larger catchment area (Figs 108, 109).

The rear buildings, tackled at the same time, were a much more difficult proposition for several reasons. The buildings were much more mixed, both in visual quality and soundness of construction; many of them had deteriorated in the long period of blight preceding The Pavements redevelopment; and the area was something of a rabbit warren. Moreover, a crucial linking element in the council's strategy for Central Pavement – a new 'magnet' store to extend the pedestrian flow of The Pavements eastwards across the pedestrianised stub of Tontine Road – had not yet been realised.

The council, owner of this area as a result of comprehensive development area purchases, nonetheless pressed ahead. Some buildings had to go, either because they were too decayed to save or impeded access, but infill has, by careful use of salvaged and other matching materials, contrived to catch the character and atmosphere of the yards (Fig 110).

The overall aim was to adapt existing buildings wherever possible and provide a cohesive shopping environment sympathetic to the traditional townscape and texture of this area. Commercially the aim was to complement the convenience shopping of The Pavements with specialist trades. In setting initial shop rents the council recognised that, until the major store unit and through pedestrian route arrived, some of the shops might have to struggle.

The refurbishment scheme, designed by the council's own architects with advice from Feilden & Mawson, dealt with the familiar problem of empty or underused storeys by linking the upper floors of both front and rear buildings to create two office suites, each with access from Theatre Yard and each soon let to insurance companies, for whose local offices they have proved very suitable. Work involved strengthening upper floors to take higher loadings and upgrading to meet the fire officer's fire resistance and escape requirements.

The scheme created 2000 sq m (21,500 sq ft) of retail and office space, and cost £486,000, of which English Heritage contributed £38,000 in section 10 grants towards repair of listed buildings. The council's Town Centre sub-committee received a feasibility report and

Fig 110 Theatre Yard, a passageway leading off Central Pavement, after restoration

approved the scheme in June 1982; work started on site, following public consultation and receipt of listed building approval, in July 1983 and was completed in February 1985.

By spring 1988 both missing elements in the Central Pavement jigsaw, Falcon Yard and the linking infill, appeared ready to fall into place. The council had agreed terms with Simons of Lincoln for a £2m development on the 'north of library' site. This scheme was to provide a store for Mothercare opening out of the Tontine Road space opposite the eastern entrance of The Pavements alongside the main entrance of the library. It would also include pedestrian steps down to Theatre Yard and, tucked in under Mothercare, several smaller shop units. The scheme promised not only to supply the missing through route east–west from The Pavements but, with the five or more new shop units, to round off the southern site of Theatre Yard. Following initial delay, construction has now started.

Falcon Yard

The final element in the revitalisation of the Central Pavement area is 'Falcon Yard' – the north–south row of buildings lying east of Theatre Yard and bounded by Falcon Yard on the west and South Street on the east. The council owned the greater part of this area but not the key buildings closest to Central Pavement proper. It and the private owner, Aureole Investments, agreed a joint development involving some commercial-conservation compromises.

Most notably, the council and its consultants urged retention for townscape reasons of the colonnaded frontage to Central Pavement; Aureole were unhappy about ending up with a shop whose window was still two metres back from the pavement edge under the first floor overhang. Eventually they accepted this, but as a quid pro quo for making what they believed to be a commercial sacrifice, the council agreed that they could demolish and redevelop to a more generous building line the adjoining red-brick nineteenth-century premises in South Street (Fig 111).

Fig 111 South Street. Western frontage undergoing restoration

74

More positively, the scheme – for which the council is using Aureole Investments' architects, Building Design Partnership – widens the middle section of Falcon Yard where it connects with Theatre Yard via an archway. This enlarged pedestrian space also connects the Falcon Yard block to South Street through a building which, visually, cries out for insertion of a prominent 'doorway'.

Overall in the Central Pavement scheme one can regret the loss of a number of buildings and features, but the 'added value', environmental as well as commercial, when this complex of lanes and squares comes fully alive promises amply to justify such compromises.

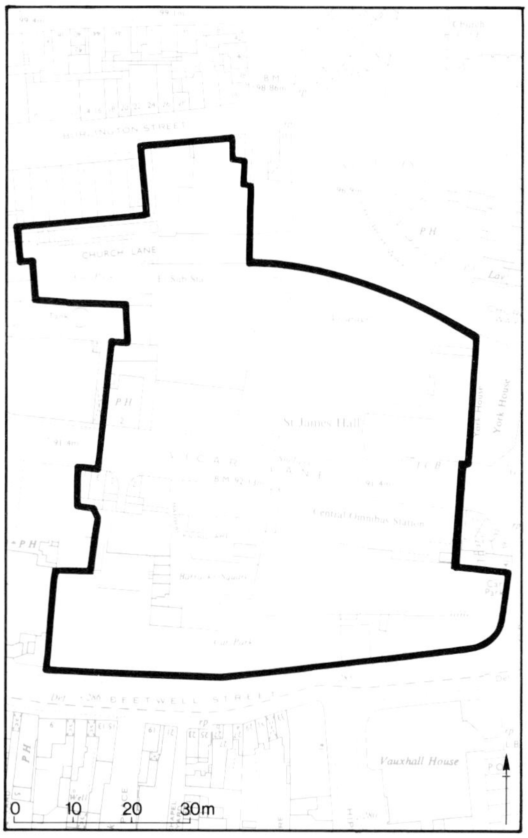

Fig 112   Scheme for the Vicar Lane shopping development prepared in 1987 by Feilden & Mawson for the Borough Council. Site Plan

Vicar Lane

The Vicar Lane site which, at the time of writing, is the latest and largest stage of town centre shopping, comprises some 2.2 hectares, 5.5 acres, east of The Shambles. It is bounded on the west by properties in Packer Row and South Street, on the north by Burlington Street, traditionally a prime shopping area, on the north-east by Church Way, on the east by St Mary's Gate, and on the south by Beetwell Street.

The land falls steeply from Burlington Street to Beetwell Street, and the brief drawn up by the council with Feilden & Mawson aims to take advantage of this. It should not only, as at The Pavements, facilitate servicing and parking arrangements, but should also help to ensure pedestrian flows throughout a three-level shopping pattern. The scheme includes two intersecting malls: east–west along the line of Vicar Lane, which is to be swallowed into the development, thus extending the pedestrian routes from the Market Place and The Pavements through Central Pavement; and north–south, connecting Burlington Street across Church Lane to intersect with the Vicar Lane mall and then, via a prominent top-lit 'hall', with a relocated mini bus station on Beetwell Street (Figs 112, 113).

The original brief aimed to make the Vicar Lane shopping achieve certain qualities which The Pavements had achieved, and also some which it had not. The development was to be respectful of and sympathetic to existing townscape; to safeguard views out from, for instance, Central Pavement to Chesterfield's surrounding hills; and, by using pitched roofs broken into relatively small elements, to safeguard the essential character of the town's roofscape as seen from those hills.

Loftier and lighter

But the brief also called for loftier, lighter, more spacious malls than CIN and their architects had felt able to provide; and commercially the emphasis of the scheme was to be on high-quality consumer durables rather than convenience purchases. This commercial character has now been reinforced by the decision of a major supermarket, after several years of discussion, to go for an out-of-town site rather than locate at Vicar Lane.

The Vicar Lane site contains two worthwhile buildings – one Georgian, one 1920s, and both unlisted. The 1920s building in Burlington Street has both intrinsic quality and is of value in giving continuity. The intention is to demolish a number of dull or thoroughly ugly buildings, notably the Woolworth store in Burlington Street (Fig 114), opened in the mid 1970s but almost certainly designed in the 1960s and typical of that period in its out-of-scale brashness, harsh materials, and lack of respect for the scale of the street. Selective demolition of bad buildings may be as important an ingredient of conservation as retention of the good.

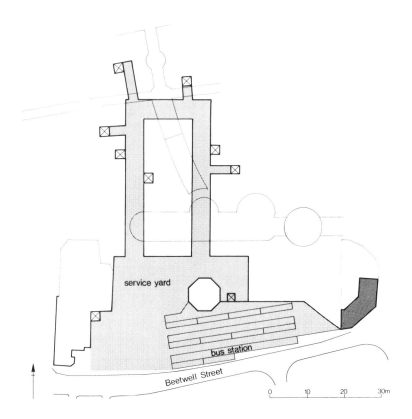

Fig 113 Feilden & Mawson's suggested treatment for the Vicar Lane shopping centre. *This page* service level and lower mall level; *facing page* upper mall level

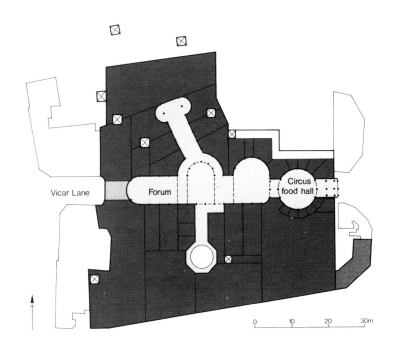

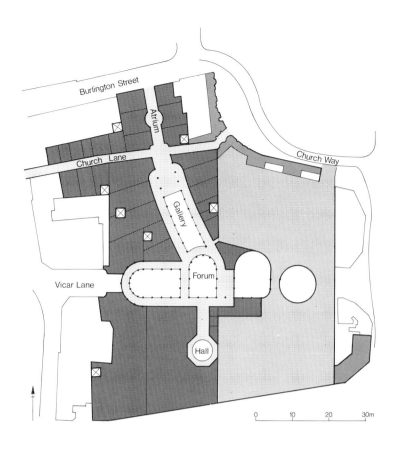

Sympathetic but different

Broadly, however, as Feilden & Mawson pointed out, the Vicar Lane site was large enough and sufficiently detached to take an architectural treatment sympathetic to but different from adjoining townscape. They suggested colonnades to give rhythm and unity externally and a Roman theme with forum, circus, and other elements freely interpreted for the interior. The latest scheme subsequently prepared by Building Design Partnership adopts the colonnades – which should be particularly valuable in the curved elevation facing St Mary's Church – but not the Roman theme. Other changes include concentration of the multi-storey car park on the southern, Beetwell Street side of the development, with office uses behind the St Mary's Gate elevations.

Fig 114   Woolworth building, Burlington Street

The overall scheme comprises some 27,000 sq m, 290,000 sq ft, of retail space (as compared with 15,000 sq m, 160,000 sq ft, in The Pavements), about 1850 sq m, 20,000 sq ft, of offices, car parking for 680 vehicles with access from Beetwell Street, bus stands on the Beetwell Street side, a replacement pub, and replacement hall and office facilities for the church. The shopping ingredient will, it is hoped, include a department store and some major quality users of the standard and appeal of Laura Ashley, Habitat, or Jaeger. Unit shops will be in the size range 2500–5000 sq ft now demanded by many retailers rather than the 1000–1500 sq ft found in The Pavements, but plans also envisage kiosks for smaller independent traders – commercially useful in helping to give life and colour to the malls.

Overcoming a snag

About three-quarters of the Vicar Lane site belonged to the council; the remainder was owned by Woolworth and by Burton Properties and developers Millards whom they absorbed. These private sector owners formed a joint company and competed with six other developers to develop the site. On the basis of interviews, the council selected the Burton/Millard/Woolworth scheme.

In the spring of 1988 the £40m scheme ran into an unexpected hurdle – the (presumably unintended) result of proposed new clauses to a Local Government Finance Bill. Chesterfield was one of a number of councils protesting that perfectly proper land transactions made in partnership with private developers were likely to be caught by provisions designed to outlaw 'creative accountancy' techniques frowned on by central government. As a result the council and its developer partner had to work out a new financial agreement to circumvent the difficulty, which was a factor in the slippage of the hoped-for timetable. By December 1988 council and developer had concluded detailed heads of agreement and expected a start on site in late 1989 with opening in 1992 – a year later than they had originally intended.

The impact of the development

The scheme by Building Design Partnership posed major townscape, archaeological, and commercial questions when it was submitted in 1989. At the time of writing (late 1989), these had yet to be resolved. The need is to reconcile the scale of development with that of the existing town centre, affording thereby a more incremental response to the continuing demand for shopping space.

The adoption of conservative estimates and an incremental approach to redevelopment has proved successful in Chesterfield's story to date and can continue to do so in the future. Indeed, these principles lie at the very root of the lessons which Chesterfield can provide for other towns.

8 Some lessons from Chesterfield

It is the conviction of the author and of English Heritage that what happened in Chesterfield has much to tell us. Its main lessons are still valid; some have not yet been learned; others are only just emerging.

Shopping guidelines

In May 1988 English Heritage, alarmed by the threatened impact of a boom in retail development on historic towns, issued a set of guidelines for developers (Fig 115). They included (see Appendix) respect for the fabric and textures of groups of buildings and spaces, not just individual listed buildings; designs minimising bulk; flexibility of future use; design competitions with public participation; separation of design competition from financial competition; avoidance of 'facadism'; care to prevent the convenience of access and deliveries destroying the fabric and character of towns; and more priority for pedestrians (who after all are the lifeblood of shopping centres), with consideration given to allowing pedestrians priority at peak shopping times where spatial segregation of vehicles and pedestrians is impracticable.

These guidelines are commendable for both their good sense and their succinctness. In principle they command a wide measure of support; in practice it will often require a great deal of determination, skill, and ingenuity to make them work. The path of the conservationist seldom runs smooth. For each hurdle successfully vaulted, removed, or circumvented, another appears. Despite a general acceptance in principle of an incremental, flexible approach to town centre redevelopment, the instinct of developers is to prefer cleared sites. They may concede all the arguments about the value of existing buildings of character in giving quality to their developments, and about the psychological importance of a degree of continuity, but too often these very valid arguments are not translated into practical attitudes and mechanisms for integrating conservation into a development timetable and budget.

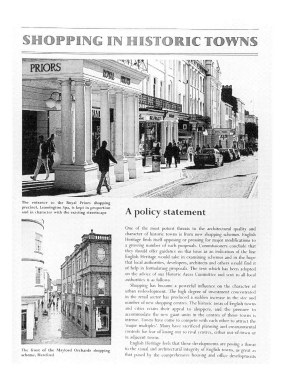

Fig 115   Leaflet prepared by English Heritage in 1988 setting out its policy and advice with respect to new shopping developments in historic towns

Good for its time

The Pavements at Chesterfield was a creditable result at the time. It achieved the required new infusion of up-to-date shopping and yet preserved the townscape (and rather more than the townscape) of Low Pavement. The shopping mall has undoubtedly been popular with shoppers, and in practical terms works well. But increasingly, as people experience the more stimulating environments of more recent covered shopping centres, they are likely to judge it dull and a little claustrophobic. If the Vicar Lane redevelopment is realised as envisaged, with lofty, multi-storey shopping malls and a sense of lightness and space, there may well be pressure for a refurbishment or face-lift to The Pavements.

In the course of researching this study, I asked both the development

79

manager (Ernie Covey, formerly of CIN) and the project architect (Duncan Studholm of Elsom Pack Roberts) whether, with hindsight, they would have wanted to do The Pavements differently. It is, I think, significant that each answered, on reflection, broadly 'No' – given the various requirements.

Mr Covey would, given the option, still have preferred a clear site without the complication of Low Pavement conservation; though he and CIN are, all things considered, reasonably happy with the commercial performance of the scheme. Mr Studholm would still have gone for a functional solution which he had confidence would work, rather than the loftier, more complex pattern of shopping malls proposed by Geoffrey Mitchell of Feilden & Mawson.

Competing in quality

This, it seems to me, presents a paradox and something of a dilemma. Retail development today operates increasingly in a climate of competition, and competition in quality. The winners are those who provide not only the most attractive retail mix but also an attractive shopping environment. Success, and indeed often survival, will – to quote but one experienced consultant, Robert McKenzie of Edward Erdman – depend in considerable measure on producing shopping environments that are convenient, agreeable, stimulating, and distinctive in character.

Yet fighting against that is the development industry's deeply-ingrained instinct not to be different but to go for a well-tried formula. 'Formula development' tends to look depressingly similar wherever it is; even if the developer tries to 'theme' it distinctively, design clichés may give the game away. Moreover 'clear-and-rebuild' over a wide area removes any sense of layered history, of the patina of decades and centuries. It also tends to remove the physical idiosyncrasies which, while inconvenient and irritating to those of tidy mind, do add the sense that here is a 'real' place.

Some lessons from Chesterfield

Many lessons can be drawn from the Chesterfield experience, some of them peculiar to that particular place and time. Here I offer a few which appear to me to be more generally applicable and valid for the future.

1   The nature of the 'prime pitch'

It has been said that in shopping development three factors are crucial: location, location, and location. In Chesterfield, as elsewhere, the initial instinct of property professionals was to interpret that criterion narrowly. The prime pitch was Burlington Street/High Street/north side of Market Place.

One group of professionals was prepared to act more boldly.The Pavements has proved them right. The area of profitable shopping can be spread if the lie of the land is right and if new and existing generators of pedestrian flow can be tied skilfully into an expanded network of pedestrian routes. In Chesterfield two of the key 'magnets' were the new car park and the existing open market.

Chesterfield shows that, by shifting the 'prime' shopping area, marginally but crucially, what at first sight appears to be the dilemma of choosing between conservation and redevelopment may often be solved by combining the two.

2   Critical mass

When a town's shopping is at least relatively speaking in decline, redevelopment of a certain minimum size may be required to start the revitalisation process. To achieve that critical mass some sacrifices may, as in Chesterfield, need to be conceded. The preferred option of incremental redevelopment/refurbishment (see 7 below) may need to be postponed until later stages. In fact in Chesterfield the new development, The Pavements, created the enhanced confidence and rental values which allowed subsequent refurbishment schemes to go ahead economically. Even so, it was based on a conservative estimate of the need for shopping space (see 4 below).

3   Need for a new 'image'

Urban regeneration is as much a psychological as a physical and economic process. Whatever is or is not done by way of redevelopment, creation of a 'new image' of the place is essential to boost morale and change the perceptions of insiders and outsiders. In principle, the refurbishment and beneficial reuse of existing buildings may be as effective a way of achieving this as clear-and-rebuild. Certainly it is likely to be less disruptive and disorientating to the community.

4   Shopping need – conservative estimate justified

The Pavements development was based on an essentially conservative projection of shopping need in the Chesterfield area. This approach paid off, though in a very negative way. The sharp and largely unexpected slump in shopping demand associated with a period of recession left the development – and its tenants – doing less well than they had hoped but much less badly than would have been the case with a more ambitious development. While others elsewhere had 'egg on their faces', Chesterfield council and CIN chalked up what was in all circumstances a reasonable return on their investment.

A recent rent review in the Pavements was also somewhat disappointing, though from the local authority's standpoint at least it represented a satisfactory rate of growth. From the funding institution's point of view, it came a year or so too early. Since then redeveloped shop premises at the corner of Farmer's Row and Vicar Lane have let at the staggering level of £60 per square foot Zone A (that is for prime space close to the street) – a 50% increase on any rental previously obtained in the town. This has implications for the main Vicar Lane development and suggests that a gradualist approach to expansion of the shopping area does in the long run pay off.

5   Conservation and redevelopment

Conservation of individual buildings as well as townscape is compatible with major redevelopment even though the methods and philosophies of clear-and-rebuild run sharply counter to those of conservation. There is, however, a case for separating the conservation elements of such a large scheme from the main new-build contract, so that the conservation skills of specialist architects and contractors can be brought to bear on the buildings to be retained. But such a solution, to be acceptable to developers, would need to be very clearly structured and subject to effective overall coordination.

6   Keeping the texture

The conservation approach adopted in Chesterfield was deliberately low-key, producing an agreeable and convincing mixture of refurbishment and infill. Retained buildings give the impression of being well cared for but not over-restored. They have the idiosyncratic appeal associated with a conservative approach to conservation. The approach may be likened to that of a good dentist – he prefers mending and reinforcing to extracting.

The result avoids being too neat and tidy. Right-angles often look a degree or two away from 90; surfaces are not excessively even. Developers and their architects need to practice self-denial in these matters, even at the risk (as happened on Low Pavement) of unknowingly burying decay which has to be removed later. If they can resist over-restoring, the result is much more attractive and has greater public appeal. The layman would say that, not being too bright and shiny, not being too smooth and rectilinear, it 'looks natural'.

7   Incremental redevelopment

An incremental, step-by-step approach to urban regeneration redevelopments is generally preferable on conservation grounds. Given the difficulties of site assembly and securing anchor tenants, funding and planning, building control, and listed building consents, it may often be also a more practical approach financially. Developers and their advisers being essentially cautious and conservative by instinct (as generally is public opinion), this has the advantage of establishing by limited, practical example what is possible in future. The successive steps should, however, slot into a clear but flexible strategy set out by the planning authority and/or the landowner.

8   Flexibility to cope with change

The shortcomings of 1960s and early 1970s shopping centres are not just environmental. They were too finite and lacked flexibility. In particular the standard unit of the 1960s and early 1970s – regarded as *de rigeur* by retailers – was 1000–1500 sq ft; today retailers increasingly demand 2500 sq ft upwards. Some flexibility can be built into structures; more flexibility should be built into the tenancy arrangements. But spreading redevelopment over a period of years in relatively small instalments can act as an insurance policy to cope with changes of fashion and requirements.

9   Gradualism and public reaction

A gradualist approach also has advantages in other respects. Chesterfield is now moving towards a more thoroughgoing pedestrianisation of the central shopping zone. This would not have been acceptable to public opinion when a measure of vehicle exclusion was first canvassed; the unfamiliar is by its nature unpalatable. But having lived with limited traffic exclusion for several years, having found it acceptable, and having discovered for themselves good reasons for a more stringent regime, shoppers and traders are more likely to support this change.

10   Design quality and competition

Retail developers now realise that they are competing for and with quality rather than quantity. They are therefore more ready to accept more interesting architectural solutions. It is noteworthy that the light, airy shopping malls which Feilden & Mawson unsuccessfully proposed for The Pavements have been accepted by the Burton consortium as both practicable and appropriate for Vicar Lane. Developers also now sense that, in a 'buyer's market', shoppers will react against the 'anywhere' shopping environment. This should help both to conserve distinctive townscapes and attractive buildings and to raise the quality of new design.

11   Firm design control

The overall shopping environment is only as good as its parts. Environmental quality depends crucially on a firm consistent design policy for street-level features such as paving, street furniture, and shop-fronts. Landlord control is in many respects more effective than planning control. In Chesterfield's case, the shortcomings of planning control are demonstrated by the case of the Collingwood shopfront at 16 High Street. Collingwood's, the county jewellers, declined to follow the council's guidance on appropriate shopfronts in this important location, appealed against refusal to allow their own design, and were upheld by the Secretary of State on the unimpressive grounds that the submitted design, while not all it ought to be, represented some improvement on the existing lamentable state of the building (Fig 116).

Where, as in Chesterfield, good shop-front design is an essential part of economic regeneration, the Department of the Environment and its inspectorate ought almost always to support the planning authority – especially when its stand is backed not only by consultants initially recommended by the Department but by local amenity societies, local architectural opinion, and other traders. Visual consistency is in such circumstances more important than a retailer's right to instal his standard or preferred style.

Fig 116   Scheme for the restoration of Colling-woods, a High Street shop, prepared by E W Simpson, Principal Architect, Chesterfield Borough Council

12   Independent advice

It has been said that organisations call in consultants to tell the decision-makers what they are unwilling to hear from their own staff. There is more than a grain of truth in that, but in Chesterfield's case the role and value of consultants has been much greater.

In the first place, the council hired them to get itself off the hook – to demonstrate that, in a changing climate, other solutions were feasible. Feilden & Mawson, as conservation consultants, started on their enormously challenging task with two unusual advantages: they had been chosen not just by Chesterfield but by a selection panel that included also the county council and the Department of the Environment; and written into their terms of reference was an unusual degree of independence. While the report of the study group was to be a collaborative effort, nothing they said about the conservation aspects could be altered without their agreement, and the costings of conservation elements of any scheme were to be their costings.

Over the years, Chesterfield has had much reason to be glad of its conservation consultants, who know the town and its buildings intimately but are also outsiders who can take a detached view and can perceive opportunities and solutions that do not always occur to those involved in a local authority's daily routine. Councillors who may at first have been sceptical of 'those folk from Norwich' have learned to look at Feilden & Mawson's advice with respect. Since the completion of the original study, they have chosen to pay for that advice without the benefit of any DoE contribution. Like the best of developers, the council regards the fees paid to its expert consultants as money well invested.

13 A wide remit

The extent of the consultants' brief is important. The council asked them to study not just a redevelopment site, nor even the main central core of the town, but the whole town centre. This has enabled them to focus on buildings and sites on the fringes of the central area and on other economic opportunities which may facilitate reuse and refurbishment or sympathetic redevelopment.

14 Attention to detail

Attention to detail in design and materials is also crucial. A town benefits from having consultants who know instinctively from training, experience, and careful study what roof pitch will work in a given situation, what brick or roofing material will look right in a given location, and how spaces as they widen, narrow, or turn lead the eye – and the shopper – on through an arch or round a corner.

We may take just two examples of Geoffrey Mitchell's contributions in Chesterfield. First, and very important because it is such a prominent building, is the design of the New Beetwell Street multi-storey car park which, instead of the once-standard horizontal layer-cake in stained concrete, is clad in brick and has a degree of vertical emphasis provided by rows of separate 'punched' window openings with decorative grills. Though large, it looks at home in the traditional townscape; its considerable bulk is broken up by brick and metalwork detailing.

Fig 117   Bridge over Elder Way linking two parts of the Co-op store

Secondly, and illustrating a sketch solution offered by the consultant and adopted by others, is the bridge across Elder Way joining the original Coop store to its eastern annexe (Fig 117). This annexe, incidentally, was originally proposed as a single-storey building, which would have blown a hole in the containing streetscape. Though by no means perfect, the annexe and bridge have repaired and reinforced the streetscape. The town centre looks as though it continues northwards instead of fizzling out.

15   The right client department

Another key element in the success of the Chesterfield experiment is the nature of the council department and officers who receive and implement the consultants' proposals and suggestions. Clearly much of this has to do with individuals and their relationship on the one hand with the consultants and on the other with leading councillors. Commitment to an overall conservation strategy needs to go hand in hand with flexibility and a degree of enlightened opportunism.

But the kind of council department is also important. In Chesterfield the key officer is responsible both for planning and for estates. This combination – whether in the form found in Chesterfield or as the more common directorate of development including planning estates and sometimes architecture – is clearly useful where conservation and economic regeneration are recognised as complementary, not conflicting, objectives.

16   Making a town come alive

The success of a conservation/economic regeneration strategy is now increasingly seen to depend not only on physical improvements and numbers of retail outlets. A town centre can be attractive to shoppers because it is alive, provides other useful services, and is a pleasant and entertaining place to spend time.

A number of diverse factors make Chesterfield a magnet that many shoppers find more compelling than larger centres such as Sheffield and

Derby. The shopping core is compact; parking and bus stops are reasonably convenient; but above all the place is lively and bustling. The open market (which the original redevelopment would have tidied away to the fringe of the shopping area) is a great draw and gains from its central location; so does the new public library with its wide range of facilities and an entrance adjoining The Pavements. The market days have extended to include a Thursday 'flea market' which in turn helps to spread shopping over the week for other traders.

The Job Centre on Low Pavement is also a focus of activity (though for some people less happily so); cafés ranging from Macdonalds on the Central Pavement/Tontine Road corner to the excellent Mr C's on Low Pavement also give people an incentive to linger in the town, a sense that being in Chesterfield is itself a pleasurable activity. Utilitarian shopping merges with leisure and tourism, and is helped by a sense that this town is a special place – a sense reinforced by the town's idiosyncrasies, such as the literally *low* pavement (a step below the road surface at one point) and the council's horse-drawn dustcart collecting market refuse on Mondays, Fridays, and Saturdays (Fig 118).

Fig 118 The Borough Council's horse-drawn dust-cart

17   Management mechanisms

Good management and maintenance of enclosed shopping centres is essential to keep them attractive and to safeguard the investment. The Pavements has been managed by its owner, the borough council, in consultation with the investor, CIN, and has worked well. But this is probably not the most promising formula for the future, for several reasons:

1   Government policies are likely, on present indications, to militate against a local authority maintaining this kind of ownership and management role.

2   A local authority may, because of central government spending constraints, be inhibited from carrying out such functions as fully as it ought to.
3   Perhaps most important, there is a need to treat whole town centre shopping zones as managed areas; and this may perhaps be best achieved not by local authority acting as such, but by local authority, property owners, and traders joining in some kind of a management trust. Advantages of such an arrangement would include potentially greater involvement of these private sector interests and a degree of insulation from public sector spending constraints.

18   The meaning of Chesterfield

Many other towns could follow Chesterfield's example – towns as little regarded as Chesterfield was at the start of our story, but each with a distinctive character and buildings and townscapes which help to make up that character. They are towns in which a conservation approach to regeneration could work successfully.

This is not to recommend a standard formula for conservation/regeneration. There can be no such thing. Rather, as Geoffrey Mitchell has stressed, Chesterfield offers a demonstration of what is possible, and a base from which to begin the hard but necessary task of identifying in each particular place what is familiar, distinctive, and of value, what the potential is of what exists, and how to build on that potential.

19   The future for Chesterfield

Chesterfield, after an all but disastrous start, has done well. It has conserved and improved on its town centre in a way that, 20 years ago, would have seemed incredible. The town's economy is more buoyant than the local economies of many other places that went faster and more full-bloodedly into redevelopment. Chesterfield is a success.

But, as those in key positions in the council realise, there is no room for complacency. Success has been built on two qualities in the town centre environment: it is attractive; and it is authentic. Those qualities depend on setting and maintaining the highest standards. Other places with a less rich heritage have been tempted to go for the ersatz – for 'Widow Twankey' townscape. Chesterfield does not need, and cannot afford, weak imitation. Whether in new buildings or in refurbishment and conversion, it can afford nothing but the best.

In applying those standards, its planners – both officers and planning committee members – have the advice of good and trusted consultants. They need the continuing support of other councillors, traders, townspeople, English Heritage, and the Department of the Environment. Design detail does matter; quality must be supported.

20   The future for shopping centres

All this has wider implications. Out-of-town and edge-of-town shopping centres have their place. But they also have their limitations. Even where their designers and developers strive to build in agreeable environments and leisure facilities, they are essentially synthetic. They bear somewhat the same relation to the real thing as instant mashed potato does to new potatoes with mint and butter – they are useful in the short term but have a distinctly limited appeal! They are in no way the ideal recipe.

Real town centres, like Chesterfield, have layers of other, often non-commercial facilities – libraries and job centres have been mentioned. They have post offices, insurance brokers, government offices, council offices, markets, and a variety of specialist or fringe shops and restaurants which, for locational as well as commercial reasons, are unlikely to set up or survive in a new out-of-town development.

So the out-of-town centre is no substitute for the real thing. With skill and care, existing town centres can recreate themselves without sacrificing either character and sense of place or this diversity of services. Who knows what the future holds for out-of-town centres? Another, more chronic energy crisis, over-provision and resultant closures in the face of a dip in the growth of retail trading – these and other factors could begin a slide away from out-of-town locations.

Real town centres are too important to be sacrificed to fluctuating retail patterns. They represent the social investment of centuries. They symbolise the community in a way that even the most glamorous green field shed never can. And in the best of them, townscape is an organic growth which should be adapted only with caution and sensitivity. It cannot be instantly recreated.

Out-of-town centres can be put up – and torn down – in months. Good town centres cannot be replaced or duplicated. They need more consideration than our society has lately been giving them. Ministers, councillors, citizens, take heed. For here is the heartbeat of the nation.

Appendix

Shopping in historic towns: a policy statement

(Sent by English Heritage Historic Areas Division to all District and County Planning Officers in England, May 1988)

1 Shopping has become a powerful influence on the character of urban redevelopment. The high degree of investment concentrated in the retail sector has produced a sudden increase in the size and number of new shopping centres. The historic areas of English towns and cities retain their appeal to shoppers, and the pressure to accommodate the new giant units in the centres of those towns is intense. Towns have come to compete with each other to attract the 'major multiples'. Many have sacrificed planning and environmental controls for fear of losing out to rival centres, either out-of-town or in adjacent towns.

2 English Heritage feels that these developments are posing a threat to the visual and architectural integrity of English towns as great as that posed by the comprehensive housing and office developments of the 1960s. The threat is particularly severe in the smaller market towns which largely escaped earlier waves of redevelopment, many of them still predominantly of a Georgian or early Victorian character.

3 We accept that shopping is the essence of a market town. It attracts people and prosperity and the town grows and changes in response to new demands. Many towns are now worried at the growth of out-of-town shopping, based on intensive car use and motorway access, and feel that they need to be able to offer 'the multiples' central sites on which to expand. They need also to offer their customers a place in which to park their cars.

4 Against this must be set the public's concern to maintain the economic variety of historic cities and towns, as well as their visual and architectural character, in the longer term. If, however, that character is sacrificed to large-scale development undertaken in response to what could be a short-term upswing in the retail investment cycle, it cannot be recovered. Once lost, historic character is irretrievable, and the town itself loses the ability to adapt in the future to a new cycle of demand, which might well include small-scale, tourist-based, specialist shopping, or town centre housing. Many historic town centres could be left as wastelands of disused retail warehouses. Many American towns are bitterly regretting the unplanned destruction of their historic centres, now that inner city investment is seeking character and variety in the urban landscape.

5 Our task is thus to accept the need for historic towns to attract investment and provide for new retail development, whilst seeking to ensure that the process does not do irreversible damage to their architectural and visual integrity. This document is an attempt to lay down general principles to that end.

6   English Heritage takes the view that very large-scale retail developments are inappropriate to the centres, at least, of smaller market towns. Not only are they vast in themselves, usually requiring the demolition of whole neighbourhoods and the elimination of variegated economic activity, but they can blight much of the rest of the town with their traffic and by drawing custom from other shops. It is virtually impossible to accommodate modern large-scale development in historic streets without losing their essential scale and character. Since evidence of over-capacity of this sort of store is starting to emerge, planning authorities have a duty to look to the longer term in assessing applications whose apparent purpose is short-term speculative gain. They should look most carefully at the wider and longer-term social costs of such investment.

7   A large number of retail stores are now coming forward for planning approval. Their scale should be kept to a minimum and their siting and access be made as respectful as possible of existing buildings and streetscape. We would draw attention to the following considerations:

a   New shopping areas should be designed to respect existing listed buildings and conservation areas, including those in towns and cities which have suffered as the result of previous phases of urban renewal. Such respect should extend beyond individual buildings and groups. The character of English historic towns derives as much from the continuity of plot sizes, the survival of back (or burgage) plots, the pattern of lanes and alleyways, and the general historic topography, which together make up the 'grain' of the town, as from the architectural styles of the buildings, the shop fronts, and the street furniture which provide the townscape. While it may not be appropriate to preserve all such features intact in every redevelopment, respect for the scale and variety they have produced is vital.

b   The external form of the structures should seek to minimise the scale and bulk of their internal volumes, while being designed to be convertible to other uses should market circumstances change. The external detailing and materials of the structures should respect the existing character of their surroundings.

c   We recommend planning authorities to encourage competitive designs for public consultation. As a first step, the deliberation involved in such competition helps to avoid mistakes being made and provides architects and developers with ideas and options for improving their schemes. Financial bids should not form part of this initial process.

d   Part of the character of a town lies not just in the facades of buildings to the streets but in their integrity as historic structures. Buildings in conservation areas, therefore, should be preserved intact wherever possible. Whilst facade preservation is preferable to wholesale demolition (and reproduction to total oblivion), there should be a presumption against 'facadism' in conservation areas.

e   Vehicular access has proved even more damaging to many small towns than retail development itself. The demand on the part of retailers for access, delivery bays, and turning circles for large European lorries and the need to supply the shops with car parking can double or treble the site area required by a shop alone. Since towns are, by their nature, generally congested places, such a destruction of townscape in the interest of extra vehicular access can swiftly become self-defeating (as many 1960s shopping centres found). It is crucial that vehicular access should be kept unobtrusive and that priority be given to pedestrian circulation and the quality of public spaces.

f   Schemes which allow the dual use of streets – for servicing or for pedestrians – separated by time should be considered. Conscious efforts should be made to improve the appearance, attraction, and use of historic buildings, streets, and areas with preference being given to people rather than to motor vehicles.

Acknowledgements

I would like to express my thanks to a number of people without whom this book could not have been written: Alfie Wood, formerly head of Historic Areas Division, English Heritage, who commissioned me to write it; his successor Mike Pearce, who encouraged me to complete it; Brian Hennessy, for his patience, good humour, and invaluable support and attention to detail; Mike Kennedy, Chesterfield's planning and estates officer, for sparing so much time, and providing information and good company; and Geoff Mitchell of the council's consultants, Feilden & Mawson, for time, information, and valuable insights.

Others to whom my thanks are due include: Ernie Covey, formerly of CIN Properties, developers of The Pavements; Councillor Bill Flanagan, leader of Chesterfield Borough Council; Peter Glossop, architect and conservationist; Dame Jennifer Jenkins, former chairman of the Historic Buildings Council and sometime Chesterfield resident; Michael Brayshaw of the Brayshaw Harrison Partnership; Michael Brearley and Alan Baggaley of Hadfield Cawkwell Davidson & Partners, architects; Roy Davidson, cheese factor and conservationist; Bill Kennerley, conservationist; Peter Gratton, Derbyshire County Librarian; the Local History Librarian at Chesterfield; Alan Hill, bookseller; Derek Latham, architect and sometime Historic Buildings Adviser, Derbyshire County Council; Maldwyn Morgan, town planner, Feilden & Mawson; the late Margaret Robinson, conservationist and widow of Graham Robinson; Tony Smith of Goddard & Smith, economic consultants to Chesterfield Council; Duncan Studholm of Elsom Pack Roberts, architects of The Pavements; members of Chesterfield Chamber of Commerce; Chesterfield shopkeepers; and others.

In addition, I should like to thank all those individuals and organisations who supplied, or permitted the use of, photographs, plans, and drawings, in particular the following: Chesterfield Borough Council (cover; Figs 10–12, 16–18, 22–24, 26–36, 40, 42–43, 52–55, 68–72, 89–90, 104, 112–13, 116); Feilden & Mawson, Chartered Architects (Fig 25); British Library Map Department (Fig 3); Chesterfield Library Local Studies Department, Derbyshire County Council, for the use of photographs and David Roberts of Chesterfield Photographic Society who prepared these for publication (Figs 4–8); Royal Commission on Historic Monuments (England) (Figs 13–14, 19–21, 37, 105–107); *Architects' Journal* (Architectural Press) (Fig 15); *Illustrated London News* Picture Library (drawing from issue of 27 June 1857) (Fig 41); Boots Ltd, Chief Architect, Design and Construction Department (Figs 45–48); Spectrum Photography, Bolsover (Fig 51); Derbyshire County Council, Architects Department (Figs 97–102); Department of the Environment, Photography Section (Figs 38–39, 44, 65–66, 91–93); English Heritage, Photography Section (frontispiece and Figs 1–2, 49–50, 56–64, 67, 73–88, 94–96, 103, 108–111, 114–15, 117–18); Ordnance Survey, reproduction of 1–1250 plans (dated 1962, 1966, 1969, and 1975) with the permission of the Controller of Her Majesty's Stationery Office (Figs 9, 12, 29–31, 89–90, 112). The drawings (Figs 10, 16, 22–24, 32, 42–43, 45–48, 52–55, 69–72, 90, 97–101, 104, 113, 116) were prepared for this publication by Amanda Patton.

Tony Aldous, Blackheath, London; September 1990